Keep it eclectic!
♥ Barbara

Small Plates
& Dainty Desserts

To the wonderful people who made this cookbook possible:

GRAPHIC DESIGNER
Bill McConnell,
Rivet Designworks

EDITOR
Carol Ann Kates,
Penny Lane Press of Colorado

PHOTOGRAPHER
John Stafford

PHOTO EDITOR
Laura Stafford

A special thank you to my husband, John, for his patience and persistence in photographing each recipe so that there will be no question about how the finished recipe should look.

And another special thank you to all of our kids, Scott, Kristin, Laura and Christopher, for your brutal honesty with recipe testing, photo critiques and cover design. Your input has been priceless.

Last but not least, an appreciative thank you to Mike Daniels (publishercoach.com) for connecting me with my editor and printer.

ECLECTIC ENTERTAINING™ - Small Plates & Dainty Desserts

Published by:
Eclectic Entertaining
9876 Clairton Way
Highlands Ranch, CO 80126
eclecticentertaining@gmail.com
eclectic-entertaining.com

ISBN 9780985788636
Library of Congress Control Number 2016953234

Printed in Aurora, Colorado
Frederic Printing

First Edition

Cover Photo, Roasted Peach Soup with Scallops, page 115

Introduction

I grew up in a household where my mother's favorite thing to make for dinner was reservations. She shrugged off the importance of learning to prepare meals by telling me, "If you can read, you can cook." Obviously, for many years I didn't think Mom could read. But, she can. Now my mother is 83, and I have become an accomplished cook. We still laugh about her lack of passion for culinary skills. It appears to skip a generation.

As a young adult, I wanted to learn to cook and took my mother's statement to heart. I could read, therefore, I could cook. I subscribed to cooking magazines and enrolled in cooking classes. Today, I am the one teaching the classes.

I absolutely love entertaining. In the summer, I entertain on our boat at Chatfield Marina. After a day of windsurfing and kayaking, we dock and I serve appetizers and a delicious grilled dinner. The sunsets are amazing there. Our pre-concert tailgate dinners at Red Rocks Amphitheater are envied by neighboring tailgaters. In the winter, I fill a backpack with the necessities and take a respite from skiing in the back bowl of Vail where we prepare lunch on communal grills—the back drop, the beautiful Rocky Mountains. This is eclectic entertaining at its finest!

My years of entertaining have taught me that advance preparation is the key to success. Nothing is worse than a frazzled host. The majority of the recipes I create can be prepared in advance. I want to enjoy the evening as much as my guests.

Because my friends continually ask for my recipes and party menus, my husband suggested I write a cookbook. My first cookbook, award-winning *Eclectic Entertaining – 15 Complete Dinner Party Menus for Busy People Who Like to Cook*, is the result of many years of developing extraordinary recipes as well as perfecting the art of entertaining.

My second cookbook, *Eclectic Entertaining – Small Plates and Dainty Desserts*, features a variety of small plates and dainty dessert recipes, the latest trend in entertaining. Both my cookbooks share the secrets I have learned for stress-free entertaining.

Barbara Stafford, the eclectic entertainer, is a wife, mother and cooking instructor living in beautiful Colorado.

Table of Contents

Vegetables, Fruits, Legumes & Grains

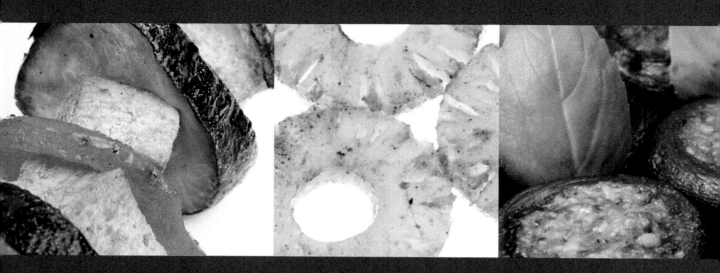

Kale Chips

Grissini

Dolmades (Stuffed Grape Leaves)

Curried Carrot Soup

Apple-Topped Acorn Squash

Grilled Onions

Basil Pesto

Marinated Sriracha Tofu Kabobs

Grilled Pineapple

Corn Pudding with Roasted Green Chiles

Mashed Cauliflower in Roasted Poblanos

Tomato Soup en Croute

Cauliflower Steaks

Pesto Stuffed Mushrooms

Veggie Bundles

Spinach Parmesan Spirals

Poblanos and Pasta

Roasted Brussels Sprouts

Stuffed Portabella Mushrooms

Stuffed Roasted Mini Peppers

Beet Bruschetta

Cheesy Pasta, Tomatoes and Herbs

Spanakopita Dumplings

Spinach Dip in Rye Bread Bowl

Mushroom Phyllo Triangles

Tomato Gazpacho

Spicy Edamame

Layered Taco Dip

Black Bean Hummus and Peaches

Roasted Red Pepper Hummus Platter

Hummus Roll-Ups

Guacamole

Vegetable Spring Rolls

Kale Chips

SERVES 6 TO 8

Healthy snack is not an oxymoron anymore. Good luck only eating a few...these are addictive!

1 large bunch (12-ounces) kale, washed, dried and stems removed

2 tablespoons extra virgin olive oil

Smoky paprika to taste

Lemon pepper to taste

Preheat the oven to 300 degrees.

Tear kale into small, chip-size pieces. Place kale pieces on a large baking sheet that has sides.

Drizzle olive oil over kale. Season to taste with paprika and lemon pepper. Toss gently, coating well. Spread kale pieces out on the baking sheet.

Bake for 30 minutes. Mix and turn kale over, baking another 20 minutes. Cool, serve. Store in an air-tight container in the refrigerator up to a week.

Grissini (Italian Breadsticks)

MAKES 25 TO 30 BREADSTICKS

Grissini are fun and quite easy to make. They have a crunchy, flavorful outside with a touch of softness in the center. These are not your mama's doughy breadsticks. You may have seen grissini in upscale restaurants served with appetizers and salads. Grace your next dinner party with them.

1 package (11-ounces) French bread dough or pizza dough

Extra virgin olive oil in a spray container

Assorted flavorings for seasoning: sea salt, lime salt, toasted sesame seeds, poppy seeds, seasoned salt, your favorite spicy seasoning, garlic powder, oregano. For a dessert twist, try cinnamon sugar.

Preheat the oven to 425 degrees. Line baking sheets with parchment paper. Roll dough out flat and place it on a cutting board. Generously spray dough with olive oil. Using a pizza cutter, cut dough into 3-inch long pieces about 1-inch wide. Place a piece of dough between the palms of your hands and rub your palms together. The dough will lengthen. Continue to roll the dough until it is the width of a thick pencil. Repeat until all pieces have been rolled.

Once dough is the desired size, place 1 tablespoon of any unsalted seasoning or 1 teaspoon of a salted flavoring on a flat plate and roll dough in seasoning, pressing seasoning into dough to ensure it sticks. Place on baking sheets about 1 inch apart and bake for 10 to 15 minutes, or until breadsticks are lightly golden. Watch closely as these can burn easily.

TIP: Symmetry is not the name of the game here. The more abstract and unalike each breadstick is the more interesting. When using salty flavorings, do not use too much or the breadsticks may be too salty.

TO SERVE: Place vertically in a pretty glass.

Dolmades (Stuffed Grape Leaves)

MAKES 20 TO 25 BUNDLES

I originally learned to make this Greek-inspired dish with beef or lamb, but the recipe evolved into this meatless one that I really love. To make it totally vegetarian, substitute vegetable broth for the chicken broth. Dolmades are guaranteed to be a crowd favorite.

FOR THE FILLING:

¼ cup extra virgin olive oil

1 large sweet onion, diced

4 garlic cloves, minced

2 cups cooked basmati rice, cooked in chicken or vegetable broth

½ cup cooked wild rice, cooked in chicken or vegetable broth

½ cup currants

½ cup fresh tomatoes, diced

¼ cup low-sodium soy sauce

½ cup fresh parsley, minced

½ teaspoon dried mint leaves, crumbled

¼ teaspoon cayenne pepper

Freshly ground black pepper to taste

In a large sauté pan, place olive oil over medium heat. Add onion and garlic and sauté until onion is limp. Add basmati and wild rice, currants, tomatoes, soy sauce, parsley, mint and cayenne and season to taste with black pepper. Stir until warmed through and thoroughly blended.

TO ASSEMBLE DOLMADES:

2 jars (15-ounces) grape leaves, rinsed in hot water to remove brine and dried on paper towels

I large lemon

Reserved lemon zest

Reserved lemon slices

6 cups chicken or vegetable broth

Dolmades continued

Using a sharp knife, trim stems from grape leaves. On a work surface, such as a cutting board, place grape leaf shiny side down. Set aside any leaves with holes as they can be used to patch holes in other leaves. If a leaf has a small hole in it, place a piece of a less-than-perfect leaf over the hole and it will seal the hole up nicely.

Place a heaping tablespoonful of filling on lower center of leaf. Begin to roll leaf up, folding stem side up over the rice mixture and then the opposite side over the mixture. Roll, tucking in sides as you roll. The finished product will resemble an eggroll. Continue until all leaves are used up, using reserved leaves to patch holes where needed.

Using a citrus zester, zest lemon and set zest aside. Using a sharp knife, slice lemon and set slices aside.

In a large sauté pan, gently place dolmades in a single layer over medium heat and cover with chicken or vegetable broth. If you need more liquid, add water. Place lemon slices over dolmades. Bring broth to a gentle boil, then reduce heat to low. Simmer dolmades covered for 45 minutes, or until dolmades are tender when pierced with a fork.

TO SERVE: Stack dolmades like a pyramid and sprinkle lemon zest over top. Dolmades may be served warm or at room temperature.

TIP: If your supermarket doesn't carry basmati rice, which is normally stocked in the rice section, you can find it at Indian or Middle Eastern markets. It is worth hunting down as it has an amazing aroma and nutty flavor.

Curried Carrot Soup

MAKES 16 4-OUNCE SERVINGS

The presentation of this soup will make your guests smile. One taste and they'll exclaim, "Delicious!" The blending of carrots, ginger and curry is spot on!

1 pound baby carrots (already peeled)

2 cups low-sodium chicken broth

¼ cup orange juice

1 teaspoon curry powder

1 ounce fresh ginger, peeled and chopped

6 ounces Romano cheese, grated

In a high-speed blender, place carrots, chicken broth, orange juice, curry, ginger and cheese and process on soup setting until the machine turns off. Or place all ingredients in a food processor and blend until smooth.

This soup should be served warmed on the stove over a low heat until it reaches the desired temperature.

TO SERVE: pour into 4-ounce glassware and garnish with a ribbon-style carrot peeling, if desired.

Apple-Topped Acorn Squash

SERVES 8

This screams FALL and is, oh, so delicious!

2 medium acorn
squash, washed

¼ cup orange juice

2 tablespoons butter, melted

1/8 cup low-sodium
chicken broth

¼ cup brown sugar

¼ teaspoon coriander

Cooking spray

Preheat the oven to 375 degrees. Using a large butcher knife, cut squash in half lengthwise. Using a spoon, scoop out seeds. Spray a baking sheet with cooking spray. Place the squash cut-side down on the baking sheet and bake for 30 -45 minutes, or until squash is tender when pierced with a sharp knife. Once squash is cooked through, remove from the oven and cool. Using a spoon, scoop out the flesh and place it in a large bowl. Add orange juice, melted butter, chicken broth, brown sugar and coriander and mix well to combine. Squash may be a little lumpy.

Spray ramekin dishes with cooking spray and spoon the acorn mixture into the ramekins.

FOR THE APPLE TOPPING:

½ tablespoon butter

2 tart apples, peeled, cored,
and cut into 1/2-inch chunks

½ cup walnuts, chopped

1/8 cup craisins (dried
cranberries)

Ground cinnamon to taste

Ground nutmeg to taste

Ground cloves to taste

1 tablespoon butter

¼ cup bread crumbs

Lower oven temperature to 350 degrees. In a sauté pan, melt butter over medium heat. Add apples, walnuts and craisins and sauté until apples are almost tender, about 6 to 7 minutes. Season the apple mixture to taste with cinnamon, nutmeg and cloves. Spoon equal amounts of the apple topping on to squash.

In a small bowl, place butter and melt in a microwave, about 30 seconds. Add bread crumbs and mix well. Spoon the bread crumb mixture on top of the apple mixture. Bake ramekins for 20 minutes, or until warm. Remove from the oven and place on a rack until cool enough to put on plates.

TO SERVE: Place ramekins on appetizer or dinner plates.

TIP: Why wash the outside of acorn squash? Because anything on the skin will enter the vegetable through the knife used to cut it. Better to be safe than sorry.

Grilled Onions

SERVES 6

Here's a fun vegetable dish that reminds me of French onion soup. It is a perfect small plate.

6 medium sweet onions

3 beef bouillon cubes, halved

3 garlic cloves, minced

6 tablespoons butter

6 ice cubes

Freshly ground black pepper to taste

Preheat the grill to 400 degrees. Using a sharp knife, slice off the bottom of onion so that is sits flat. Slice an inch off the neck and peel onion.

Using a grapefruit knife, core out enough of the center to hold ½ bouillon cube, garlic, ice cube and butter. Reserve the center for another use.

Into the cavity, place in this order: ½ bouillon cube, ½ garlic clove, 1 ice cube, and 1 tablespoon butter. Using a finger, smooth the butter across the top evenly. Season to taste with pepper. Repeat steps for remaining onions.

Place onions on a grill pan or foil and cook, covered, 45 minutes. Serve warm.

Basil Pesto

MAKES ½ CUP

Homemade pesto is really easy and the flavor is amazing.

1 cup fresh basil leaves lightly packed

1 tablespoon toasted pine nuts

2 tablespoons freshly grated Parmesan cheese

2 tablespoons extra virgin olive oil

1 garlic clove

1/8 teaspoon freshly ground black pepper

Into the bowl of a food processor, mix basil leaves, toasted pine nuts, Parmesan cheese, extra virgin olive oil, garlic clove and black pepper. Whirl until blended and slightly chunky. If a really smooth pesto is desired, mix until it is thoroughly blended and uniform in appearance. Pesto will stay fresh covered in refrigerator for one week or frozen for three months in an airtight container.

TIP: To toast pine nuts (pignolis), heat a small frying pan to a medium heat. Add nuts only and turn until slightly browned on all sides. Remove from heat and cool before using in recipe.

Marinated Sriracha Tofu Kabobs

SERVES 6 TO 8 DEPENDING ON SKEWER SIZE

Full disclosure – the Sriracha® sauce gives this dish some heat. But, it will turn anyone into a tofu fan.

¼ cup Sriracha® Chile Sauce

½ cup low-sodium soy sauce

3 tablespoons sesame oil

2 tablespoons sweet onion, minced

Freshly ground black pepper to taste

1 package (14-ounces) extra firm tofu, drained and cut into 1-inch cubes

1 red or yellow bell pepper,

seeded and cut into 1-inch squares

1 zucchini, sliced into ¼-inch thick disks

Cooking spray for prepping grill

In a large bowl, combine Sriracha®, soy sauce, sesame oil, sweet onion and freshly ground pepper to taste. Mix well. Add tofu, zucchini and bell pepper and toss to coat well. Cover and marinate in the refrigerator overnight.

Spray the grill with cooking spray. Then, heat the grill to medium.

Onto 6 or 8-inch skewers, thread tofu, zucchini, and bell pepper, and vegetables, alternating for a colorful affect, reserving sauce to brush on while grilling. Discard marinade once kabobs are finished cooking.

Grill kabobs about 3 minutes per side, vegetables and tofu darken.

TIP: Chose the skewer length depending on the portions. Use 6-inch skewers if hosting a small plate party, and this is one of many special bites. Use 12-inch ones if this is the main event and you are serving it over your favorite rice. Either way, this dish will disappear. Even people who say they don't like tofu, love this preparation.

Grilled Pineapple

SERVES 5

1 can (20-ounces) sliced pineapple in its own juice, yields about 10 slices

¼ cup reserved pineapple juice
¼ cup honey
1 tablespoon Sriracha®

¼ teaspoon Chinese five-spice powder
1/8 teaspoon ground cloves

Drain pineapple, reserving ¼ cup of juice. In a flat dish, place pineapple slices so they do not overlap. In a medium bowl, combine pineapple juice, honey, Sriracha®, Chinese five-spice and cloves. Pour the pineapple juice mixture over pineapple slices, coating well and turning to coat both sides. Marinate an hour or until ready to grill, which can be several hours if necessary.

Preheat the grill to medium. Remove pineapple slices from the marinade. Grill pineapple slices about 5 minutes per side, brushing marinade over tops while grilling.

TIP: You can use fresh pineapple for this recipe if you wish but it is more difficult to get perfect rings.

Corn Pudding with Roasted Green Chiles

MAKES 1 LOAF

This recipe is an updated version of the corn pudding my grandmother used to make. Obviously, I loved it and still do!

¼ cup cornmeal

2 large eggs, beaten

1 can (14.75-ounces) cream-style corn

1 can (15.25-ounces) whole kernel corn

1 can (4-ounces) roasted green chiles, drained and chopped

½ cup milk

1 teaspoon melted butter

2 tablespoons all-purpose, unbleached flour (gluten free also works)

1 teaspoon sugar

¼ teaspoon sea salt or kosher salt

Basil leaves for garnishing individual servings

Preheat the oven to 350 degrees. In a large bowl, combine cornmeal, eggs, cream-style and whole kernel corn, green chiles, milk, butter, flour, sugar and salt. Pour the batter into an ungreased loaf pan and bake for 45 minutes, or until the center is firm. Top each serving with basil leaf for garnish.

Mashed Cauliflower in Roasted Poblanos

SERVES 8

Do you love mashed potatoes but feel guilty eating them?
Mashed cauliflower can be just as tasty without all the guilt.

8 poblano (pasilla) peppers

Cooking spray for prepping peppers

2 medium heads cauliflower, leaves removed and broken into equally-sized pieces

Extra virgin olive oil

3 garlic cloves

½ cup mascarpone cheese

1 cup Parmesan or Romano cheese, grated

¼ cup milk

Seasoned salt to taste

White pepper to taste

Freshly ground black pepper to taste

Paprika for garnish

Preheat the oven broiler. Lay peppers on their sides. Using a paring knife, cut an oblong shape in the side of each pepper. Reserve cut pepper piece for another use. Remove seeds but leave stems intact. On a baking sheet, place peppers cut side down and spray skins lightly with cooking oil spray. Broil for 5 minutes. Place in a paper bag and cool for 30 minutes. Peel off only loose skin.

Add an inch or two of water to a saucepan with a cover. Insert a steamer basket into the saucepan and place pan over a high heat. Bring water to a boil. When you hear water boiling and see steam coming from the pan, place cauliflower in steamer basket. Cover and steam cauliflower until very soft, about 15 minutes.

Preheat the oven to 350 degrees. In a small skillet, place olive oil over medium heat. Add garlic and sauté until garlic is golden.

In a food processor, place cauliflower, garlic, mascarpone cheese, Parmesan cheese, milk, seasoned salt, white and black peppers. Add in stages as it may not all fit at once. Process until smooth like mashed potatoes.

Using a spoon, fill the pepper shells with the cauliflower mixture and sprinkle with paprika for garnish. Place the filled peppers on an ungreased baking sheet and bake for 10 to 15 minutes, or until hot. There will be remaining cauliflower to enjoy another night.

Tomato Soup en Croute

MAKES 14 TO 16 SERVINGS

This is a meal in itself and a very good one at that.

½ cup butter, salted

1 large yellow onion, chopped

2 ½ pounds ripe tomatoes, chopped

6 cloves garlic

1 can (6-ounces) tomato paste

2 bay leaves

1 teaspoon dried thyme leaves

½ tablespoon freshly ground black pepper

4 cups half-and-half

2 tablespoons butter, salted

½ teaspoon ground white pepper

Kosher or sea salt to taste

1 package (17.3-ounces) frozen puff pastry, thawed in the refrigerator

1 large egg, beaten

In a Dutch oven, melt butter over medium heat. Add onion and sauté for 5 minutes, or until onion is limp. Add tomatoes, garlic, tomato paste, bay leaves, thyme and black pepper. Simmer uncovered until tomatoes and onions are soft, about 40 minutes. Remove bay leaves and discard.

In a food processor, place the tomato mixture and process until well blended. Return the tomato mixture to the Dutch oven. Add half-and-half, butter, white pepper and season to taste with salt. Increase the heat to medium high and bring to a boil. Turn off the heat and cool the soup on top of the stove until cool enough to refrigerator. Cover and refrigerate overnight.

Preheat the oven to 450 degrees. Using a rolling pin, roll sheets of puff pastry out until flat and larger. Place ramekins on pastry sheet. Using a sharp knife, cut 1 circle slightly larger than the ramekin for each ramekin. In 4 to 6-ounce ramekins, ladle soup. Using a pastry brush, brush 1 side of each circle with egg and place that side down over soup. Pull sides taut and press to secure pastry around dish like a little drum. Gently brush the top of pastry with egg.

Place ramekins on a jellyroll pan and bake 15 minutes, or until the crust is golden brown. Serve immediately with a side salad.

TIP: I like the lighter half-and-half; but if you are a heavy cream kind of cook, by all means use it.

Cauliflower Steaks

SERVES 2

If a grill isn't handy, you can roast the steaks in the oven at 350 degrees for 10 minutes.

1 head cauliflower

Butter-flavored extra virgin olive oil

Paprika to taste

Garlic powder to taste

Sea salt or Kosher salt to taste

Remove the leaves from cauliflower and trim the stem end so it sits flat. Place cauliflower on a cutting board with stem side facing upwards. Using a sharp knife, cut head vertically into 2 steak slabs approximately ½ to ¾-inches in thickness. Save remaining cauliflower pieces for another use.

Brush both sides of steaks with olive oil, then sprinkle with paprika, garlic powder and salt.

Preheat the grill to 350 degrees (medium heat) and cook steaks for 5 minutes, turn and cook an additional 5 minutes on the second side, or until browned.

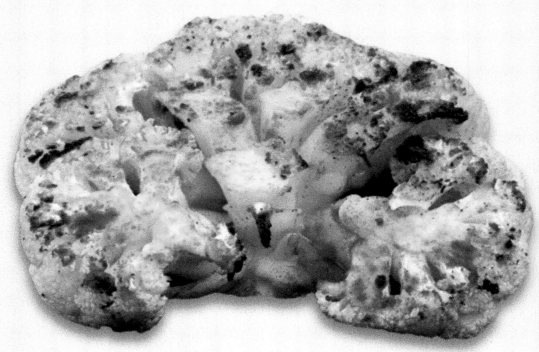

Pesto-Stuffed Mushrooms

MAKES ABOUT 15 MUSHROOMS

This recipe is so easy I am almost embarrassed when I share it. But, most of us are looking for fast, easy recipes that are also delicious. Making your own pesto gives it a more made-from-scratch touch.

8 ounces fresh white
mushrooms, washed and dried

½ cup prepared basil pesto

Preheat the oven to 350 degrees. Using a paring knife, remove stems from mushrooms and reserve for a later use. Spoon pesto into each mushroom's cavity so pesto is level with the edges. Place filled mushroom caps in an ungreased, ovenproof dish and bake for 15 minutes. Serve warm.

TIP: See Basil Pesto recipe on page 15 to make your own.

Veggie Bundles

MAKES 24 BUNDLES

Colorful, tasty and too cute for words. What are you waiting for?

FOR THE FILLING & VEGGIES:

1 container (8-ounces) mascarpone cheese

1/2 cup Romano cheese, grated

Zest of 1 lime

Juice of 1 lime, about 2 tablespoons

½ teaspoon garlic powder

¼ teaspoon freshly ground black pepper

1 zucchini, julienned 3-inches long

1 red bell pepper, seeded and cut into long, thin strips,

3-inches long

1 yellow bell pepper, seeded and cut into long, thin strips, 3-inches long

½ red onion, sliced thinly into 3-inch pieces

In a medium bowl, combine mascarpone, Romano cheese, lime zest, lime juice, garlic powder and pepper. Cover and refrigerate until ready to assemble bundles. Keep prepped veggies refrigerated until ready to assemble bundles.

TO ASSEMBLE BUNDLES:

1 package (17.3-ounces) frozen puff pastry, thawed

Reserved cheese filling

Reserved veggies

Milk for brushing

Preheat the oven to 400 degrees. On a large, flat surface and using a rolling pin, roll puff pastry into two large rectangles. With a butter knife, cut each rectangle into 12 squares yielding a total of 24 pieces. Using a small spatula, gently lift pastry up to loosen it from the flat surface.

Using a spoon, place a heaping tablespoon of the cheese mixture in the center 1 pastry square. Lay 2 pieces of zucchini, 2 pieces red bell pepper, 2 pieces yellow bell pepper and 2 pieces red onion across the top of the cheese, corner to corner. Bring all 4 corners up and press them together so that they overlap and seal the bundle together, pressing a little to secure. Repeat with remaining ingredients until all bundles are assembled. On a baking sheet lined with parchment paper, place veggie bundles. Using a pastry brush, brush bundles with milk to help them brown nicely. Bake for 17 minutes, or until golden brown. Serve warm.

TIP: Be sure to thaw the puff pastry in the refrigerator for 6 to 8 hours. If left on the counter to thaw, the pastry may stick to itself and be very difficult to separate.

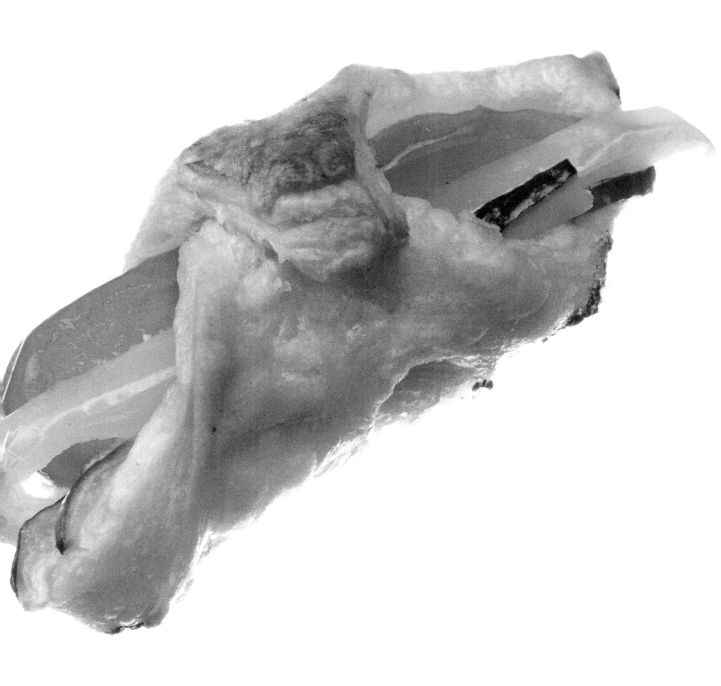

Spinach and Parmesan Spirals

MAKES ABOUT 20 SPIRALS

I created this tasty treat on the fly for a potluck Super Bowl party. I had to make do with what I had on hand. When you make this one, get creative and use the veggies and cheese you have on hand.

1 sheet frozen puff pastry

1 package (10-ounces) frozen spinach, thawed, squeezed dry and chopped

1 cup freshly grated Parmesan cheese

¼ cup pitted black olives, chopped

¼ cup slivered almonds, toasted and coarsely chopped

2 tablespoons red onion, chopped

1 clove garlic, minced

¼ teaspoon ground nutmeg

Freshly ground black pepper to taste

Milk for brushing pastry

Preheat the oven to 400 degrees.

Thaw frozen pastry sheet on waxed paper on the countertop, about 30 minutes. When thawed, using a rolling pin, roll pastry to flatten and enlarge.

In a large bowl, combine spinach, Parmesan cheese, olives, almonds, onion, garlic and nutmeg and season to taste with pepper. Using a knife, spread the spinach mixture thinly over entire pastry. Roll pastry up tightly beginning at wider end. With fingers moistened in water, seal end. Using a sharp knife, cut roll into ½-inch thick spirals. On a baking sheet lined with parchment paper, place spirals so they lay flat.

Using a pastry brush, brush pastry tops and sides lightly with milk. Bake for 15 minutes, or until pastry is golden. Serve warm.

TIP: Toasting nuts is really easy. They have plenty of natural oil. Place in a small skillet over medium heat and stir every 30 seconds or so until they start to brown. How toasted you make them is personal preference. I like mine on the well-done side.

Poblanos and Pasta

SERVES 8

One stuffed pepper serves one person. If you don't need eight servings, prep only the number of peppers you need. Don't decrease the ingredients for the pasta because it is delicious all by itself.

8 ounces penne pasta

8 poblano (pasilla) peppers

1 wheel (7-ounces) Brie, rind intact, cubed

4 ounces mascarpone cheese

2 tablespoons butter-flavored olive oil

or

2 tablespoons butter

¼ cup almonds, toasted and coarsely chopped

1 teaspoon fresh chives, chopped

¼ teaspoon nutmeg

¼ teaspoon smoky paprika

Freshly ground black pepper to taste

Preheat the oven to 350 degrees. Fill a large, heavy dutch oven with water and place over high heat. Bring water to a boil, add pasta and cook al dente according to package directions.

While pasta is cooking, using a paring knife, cut a canoe-shaped section out of each pepper. (See photo.) Reserve cut-out pepper pieces for another use. Remove seeds from peppers, leaving stem intact. Set peppers aside.

Drain water from pasta, turn the burner to off and return pasta to the kettle. Add Brie, mascarpone, olive oil, almonds, chives, nutmeg and paprika and season to taste with pepper. Mix to combine.

Fill each pepper with 1/8 of the pasta mixture and place peppers in an ungreased, ovenproof baking dish. Bake for 20 minutes, or hot. Serve hot.

TIP: Toasting nuts is easy. Just place nuts in small frying pan, heat to medium heat and toss often to avoid burning. Cool. No oil is necessary as they have enough natural oil.

Roasted Brussels Sprouts

SERVES 8 AS A VEGETABLE DISH OR MORE AS SMALL PLATES

I never thought I liked Brussels sprouts until I created this recipe. Now, I can't make it often enough; and, what I love most, it is really easy.

2 pounds fresh Brussels sprouts

2 red apples, unpeeled, cored and thinly sliced

½ sweet onion, thinly sliced

½ cup craisins

½ cup walnuts, coarsely chopped

¼ cup extra virgin olive oil

Turmeric to taste

Kosher or sea salt to taste

Freshly ground black pepper to taste

Aged-balsamic vinegar to taste for drizzling

Preheat the oven to 400 degrees. Using a paring knife, slice off ends of Brussell sprouts and cut each sprout in half, reserving any leaves that fall off.

In a large bowl, combine Brussels sprouts and reserved leaves, apple slices, onion, craisins and walnuts. Drizzle the Brussels sprouts mixture with olive oil and stir to coat evenly. Season to taste with turmeric, salt and pepper. In a jellyroll pan, spread out the Brussels sprouts mixture. Roast for 30 minutes, stirring every 10 minutes. Remove vegetables from the oven and drizzle lightly with aged-balsamic vinegar. Serve hot.

TIP: The loose leaves will caramelize more than the sprouts, which is fine, and makes for some crunchy and tasty bites.

TIP: Craisins are dried cranberries, offering a sweet and tart flavor at the same time.

Trivia: Brussels sprouts are a member of the cabbage family and have long been popular in Brussels, Belgium, where this healthy veggie likely acquired its name. Brussels sprouts are high in Vitamins A and C.

Stuffed Portabello Mushrooms

SERVES 4

A portabello mushroom makes the perfect platform for this yummy spinach stuffing.

4 portabello mushrooms, wiped clean

2 tablespoons coconut oil

1 poblano pepper, seeded and chopped

¼ cup white onion, chopped

1 large clove garlic, minced

6 ounces fresh baby spinach leaves

¼ teaspoon ground nutmeg, fresh if possible

¼ teaspoon ground turmeric

Juice of ½ lemon, about 1 ½ tablespoons

¼ teaspoon ground white pepper

Sea salt to taste

Freshly ground black pepper to taste

4 ounces cream cheese

Using a paring knife, remove stems of mushrooms and chop into ¼-inch pieces. Gently run a spoon on the underside of mushroom caps, scraping out the gills. In a medium skillet, place coconut oil over a medium heat. Add pepper, onion and garlic and sauté until onion is limp. Add spinach leaves and mushroom stems, reduce heat to low and cover. Stir occasionally and cook until spinach is limp, about 5 minutes.

Preheat the oven to 375 degrees. Season the spinach mixture with nutmeg, turmeric, lemon juice and white pepper and season to taste with salt and black pepper. Remove the skillet from the heat and thoroughly blend in cream cheese.

Place mushroom caps in an ungreased ovenproof dish. Using a spoon, divide the spinach mixture evenly between the caps, mounding the mixture up in the center.

Place in the oven and cook for 5 minutes, or until both mushrooms and the filling are warm. Serve stuffed mushrooms on small plates with forks.

TIP: This is another good recipe for your vegetarian, gluten free guests.

Stuffed Roasted Mini Peppers

MAKES ABOUT 15 PEPPERS

This is another one of my favorites that can be made ahead. The roasted garlic paired with the roasted peppers has a "wow" effect on guests. I love watching them bite into one of my stuffed peppers and hear them utter, "Yum".

15 vine sweet mini peppers

Cooking spray

2 whole garlic heads

Extra virgin olive oil for drizzling

Sea salt to taste

Freshly ground black pepper to taste

½ cup mascarpone cheese

½ cup finely grated Romano or

Parmesan cheese

½ teaspoon seasoned salt

½ teaspoon freshly ground black pepper

Paprika for garnishing

Preheat the oven to 400 degrees. Using a paring knife, slice the top ¼-inch off peppers and remove seeds. In a mini muffin pan, place peppers cut side down and spray peppers with cooking spray. Using a sharp knife, slice ¼-inch off the top end (the end opposite the root) of each garlic head, exposing cloves. In a cast iron garlic roaster, place garlic head. Drizzle with olive oil and season to taste with salt and pepper. If you don't have a garlic roaster, drizzle garlic head with olive oil, season to taste with salt and pepper and wrap in aluminum foil.

Place peppers and garlic in the oven and roast for 15 minutes. Remove peppers from the oven and cool in the pan. Continue roasting garlic for an additional 30 minutes. Remove garlic from the oven. Using a paring knife, remove cloves of garlic from heads and discard outer skin.

In a medium bowl, place garlic cloves. Using a spoon, mash cloves. Add mascarpone, Romano cheese, salt and pepper and stir to combine. Using a spoon, place the cheese mixture in the peppers, stuffing peppers level with opening. Sprinkle the cheese mixture with paprika. Serve at room temperature.

TIP: The roasted garlic is what pulls these flavors together, so don't substitute it to save time. You will see what I am talking about.

TIP: Make these 24 hours ahead and store in refrigerator in airtight container. Bring to room temperature to serve.

Beet Bruschetta

MAKES 15 TO 20 SERVINGS

This bruschetta is pretty and may be prepared in advance. Flavor? Oh, yeah—a total winner!

FOR THE BEET MIXTURE:

4 large beets

¼ cup extra virgin olive oil

2 tablespoons lemon juice

1 tablespoon lemon zest

1 ½ tablespoons
Dijon mustard

¼ teaspoon salt

¼ teaspoon ground
black pepper

Preheat the oven to 350 degrees. Cut off beet greens and either discard or wash them, place in a plastic bag, and refrigerate for another use. Scrub beets with a vegetable brush. Using a vegetable peeler, peel beets. Using a sharp knife, cut beets into quarters. Place beets in an oven-proof glass dish and roast 45 to 60 minutes, or until beets can be easily pierced with a sharp knife. Remove from the oven and cool completely. When

beets are cooled, using a sharp knife, cut beets into ¼ inch cubes.

In a medium bowl, combine extra virgin olive oil, lemon juice, lemon zest, mustard, salt and pepper. Add beets to the olive oil mixture and toss gently to coat.

TO ASSEMBLE THE BRUSCHETTA:

1 baguette, baked and sliced
on the diagonal

4 ounces mascarpone cheese

Your favorite salad greens

To build the bruschetta, spread each slice of bread with mascarpone cheese. Top each slice with salad greens and then with the beet mixture.

Cheesy Pasta, Tomatoes and Herbs

SERVES 8 TO 10

*This pasta dish is light and flavorful and explodes with fresh vegetable flavors!
Think of it as another delicious version of Pasta Primavera.*

4 ripe tomatoes, peeled, cored and chopped

½ cup frozen peas, cooked per package directions

2 tablespoons capers, rinsed and drained

½ cup extra virgin olive oil

½ cup Romano or Parmesan cheese, grated

½ cup fresh mozzarella cheese, cubed

¼ cup fresh basil leaves, chopped

1 tablespoon dried oregano leaves

¼ teaspoon sugar

1 clove garlic, minced

Sea salt to taste

Freshly ground black pepper to taste

1 package (16-ounces) penne pasta

Into boiling water, blanch tomatoes (see tip below) for one minute, remove, rinse under cold water. Peel off skin. Chop tomatoes and place in a large bowl. Add peas, capers, olive oil, Romano/Parmesan and mozzarella cheeses, basil, oregano, sugar, garlic, salt and pepper and stir to combine. Cover with plastic wrap or place in an airtight container and refrigerate overnight.

When ready to prepare pasta, remove the tomato mixture from the refrigerator. Cook penne pasta al dente according to package directions and drain. Place pasta in a large serving bowl. Add the tomato mixture and toss until blended. Serve warm or at room temperature.

Tip on peeling/blanching tomatoes: Using a sharp knife, core and make an X on the bottom of tomatoes. Drop tomato into boiling water for 10 seconds and remove. Peel tomatoes and immerse in icy cold water to retard cooking.

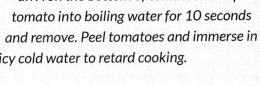

Spanakopita Dumplings

MAKES 31 DUMPLINGS

Greek-inspired filling inside an Asian dumpling because I'd rather boil than fry.

FOR THE SPINACH FILLING:

2 tablespoons avocado oil

1/3 cup sweet onion, chopped

1 clove garlic, minced

1 package (10-ounces) frozen spinach, thawed and squeezed dry

4 ounces crumbled feta cheese

¼ cup Kalamata olives, chopped

2 tablespoons lemon juice

½ teaspoon dried dill

¼ teaspoon ground nutmeg

½ teaspoon freshly ground black pepper

In a large skillet, heat avocado oil over a medium heat. Add onion and garlic and sauté until onion is limp. Add spinach to the skillet and stir to combine.

Turn off the heat and add feta cheese, olives, lemon juice, dill, nutmeg and pepper. Blend well.

TO PREPARE THE DUMPLINGS:

1 package (14-ounces) round dumpling wrapper

On a flat surface like a cutting board, place 1 dumpling wrapper. Using a spoon, drop 1 tablespoon of the spinach filling into the center of the wrapper. With wet fingers, gather the sides of the dumpling around the filling and pinch the top closed, twisting it a little to secure. Continue until all dumpling filling has been used.

Fill a large kettle with water and place over a high heat. Bring water to a boil, gently add the dumplings and boil for 3 minutes, stirring occasionally to keep from sticking. Using a large slotted spoon, remove dumplings and place on a decorative plate. Serve warm.

TIP: Round dumpling wrappers are found in Asian markets.

Spinach Dip in Rye Bread Bowl

MAKES 1 LARGE BREAD BOWL OF DIP

Even people who don't like spinach, love this dip. If you have any leftovers, my spinach dip is delicious over pasta or it makes a great stuffing for baked potatoes.

3 packages (10-ounces) frozen spinach, thawed & squeezed dry

1 cup light mayonnaise

1 can (10.75-ounces) condensed cream of mushroom soup

1 can (8-ounces) water chestnuts, drained & chopped

1 egg, hard-cooked and chopped, optional

1 tablespoon fresh lemon juice

½ teaspoon dried dill weed

Dash ground nutmeg, less than 1/8 teaspoon

Sea salt to taste

Dash white ground pepper, less than 1/8 teaspoon

Freshly ground black pepper to taste

1 round loaf of rye bread

In a large bowl, combine spinach, mayonnaise, soup, water chestnuts, egg, lemon juice, dill, nutmeg, salt and white and black peppers. Cover and chill in the refrigerator until ready to serve.

Using a bread knife, slice off the top of bread and set aside. Using a small paring knife, hollow out the insides of bread, leaving a ½-inch thick shell. Cut the removed bread into 1-inch cubes.

Using a spoon, scoop dip into the bread bowl and serve on large platter with bread cubes surrounding bowl. Additional dippers may be used as well.

SUGGESTED DIPPERS:

Baby carrots   Sliced zucchini   Snow peas

TIP: This dip may be made 24 hours before it is served. If the bread is scooped out and cubed in advance, store the bread bowl and cubes in an air-tight container to keep them moist. Otherwise, prepare the bread bowl just before serving. If you want to prepare this as single servings, use individual rolls and prep the rolls just like the bread.

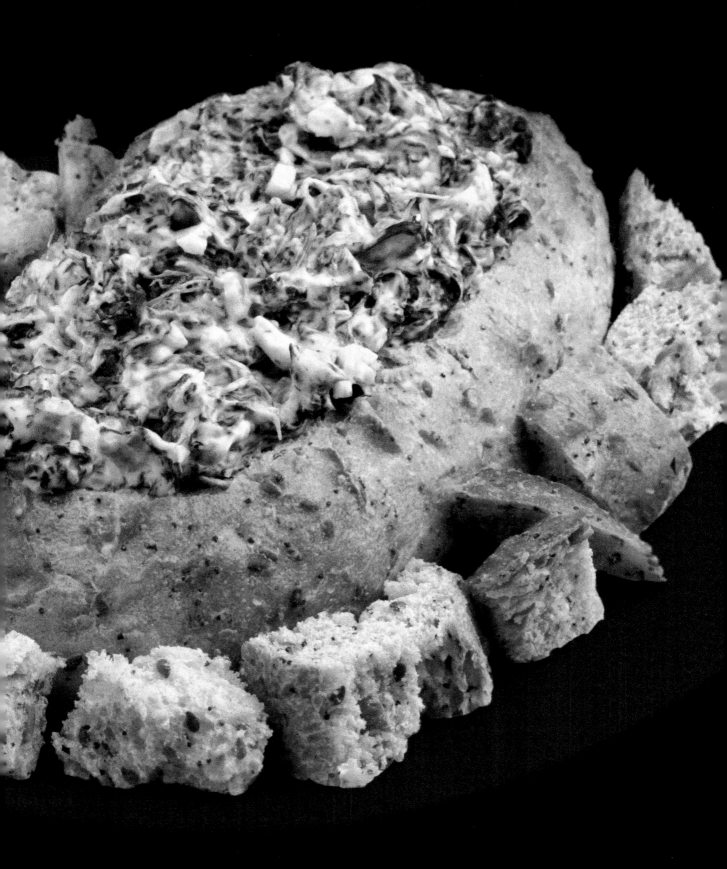

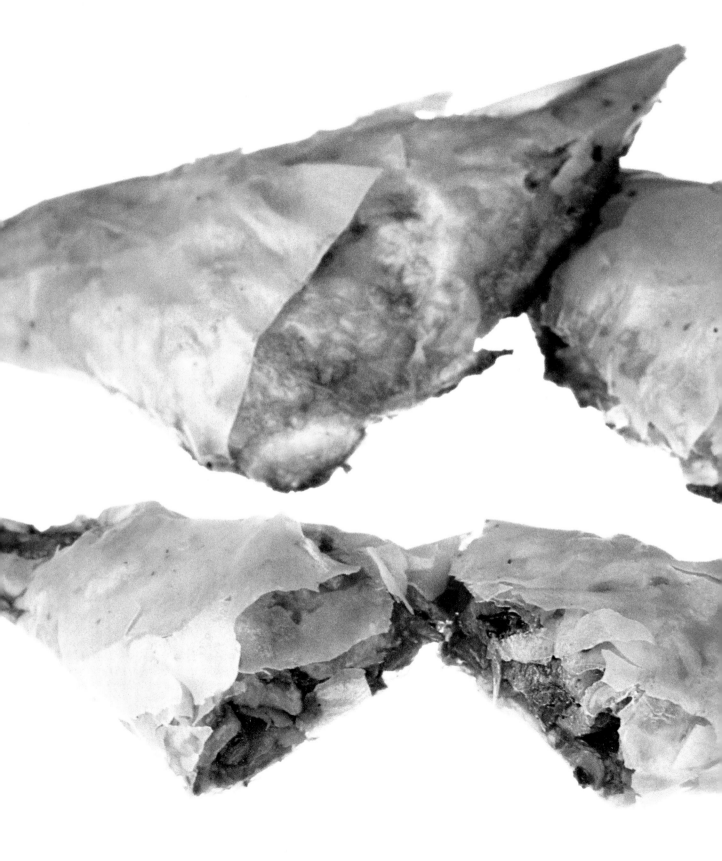

Mushroom Phyllo Triangles

MAKES ABOUT 82 APPETIZERS

These take a little time but are worth the effort. If you don't feel like making all the triangles, use the extra mushroom mixture over pasta. Most things work well over pasta in my kitchen.

4 tablespoons butter

3 pounds mushrooms, any combination of types, washed and thinly sliced

4 shallots, minced

4 tablespoons fresh thyme leaves, chopped

1 ½ teaspoons salt

½ teaspoon white pepper

1 teaspoon freshly ground pepper

½ cup cream sherry

1 ½ cups cream

3 boxes phyllo dough, thawed slowly in refrigerator (not on counter or it will stick together)

3/4 cup melted butter

In a very large skillet, melt 4 tablespoons butter over a medium heat. Add mushrooms, shallots and thyme and stir to combine. Add salt, white and black pepper and continue sautéing, stirring occasionally, until mushrooms are browned, about 5 minutes. Add sherry and cook until sherry is reduced and a glaze forms on the bottom of the pan. Add cream and continue cooking until cream thickens, coating the mushrooms well. Remove the mushroom mixture from the heat.

Using a rubber spatula, spread the mushroom mixture thinly on a jellyroll pan, cover and chill in the refrigerator until cold and thick, about 2 hours.

Preheat the oven to 350 degrees. Lay 1 sheet of phyllo dough on a nonstick surface. Cover remaining phyllo with damp paper towels to prevent them from drying out. Using a pizza cutter, cut 2 to 3-inch wide strips of dough from the shorter side. Using a spoon, place 1 tablespoon of the mushroom mixture at the bottom of a strip of dough. Using a pastry brush, brush entire strip lightly with melted butter. Fold 1 corner of edge over mixture, forming a triangle. Continue folding back and forth into a triangle until you reach the end of the strip. Brush edges with melted butter to seal up the triangle. Repeat until all the mushroom mixture has been used. Place triangles on an ungreased baking sheet and bake about 18 minutes, or until brown. Serve warm.

TIP: Reduction of the sherry is to boil until liquid has evaporated, resulting in an intense flavor and thicker mixture.

Tomato Gazpacho

MAKES ABOUT EIGHT CUPS

Enjoy on a warm summer evening with a baguette so no soup is wasted.

3 pounds tomatoes, chopped (not seeded)

1 ½ cucumbers, peeled, seeded and chopped

1 avocado, peeled, seeded and chopped

1 red bell pepper, seeded and chopped

3 green onions, chopped

¼ cup sun-dried tomatoes, chopped

1 cup Fritos® brand Original Corn Chips

¼ cup extra virgin olive oil, basil olive oil if available

2 tablespoons cream sherry

Juice of 1 lemon, about 3 tablespoons

2 cloves garlic

2 teaspoons fresh parsley

½ teaspoon fresh thyme leaves

2 teaspoon kosher or sea salt

Freshly ground black pepper to taste

Basil leaves for garnish

1 baguette, sliced in ½-inch slices

In a high-speed blender, place tomatoes, cucumbers, avocado, red bell pepper, green onions, sun-dried tomatoes, Fritos®, olive oil, sherry, lemon juice, garlic, parsley, thyme and salt and season to taste with pepper. Process until blended well with small chunks visible. Cover and chill 4 hours. Serve in 4-ounce glasses with a leaf of basil to garnish.

TIP: The avocado creates a creamier texture but is not essential if a ripe one isn't available. If your guests are gluten-free, the Fritos® are made from corn and contain no wheat. Use cream sherry in this recipe, not cooking sherry.

Spicy Edamame

SERVES 4-6

The Sriracha® gives this recipe some kick. Tone it down to suit your guests. Fresh ginger and garlic are a special treat, so don't use anything but fresh.

1 package (12-ounces) frozen edamame

2 tablespoons low-sodium soy sauce

2 tablespoons Sriracha® hot sauce

2 cloves garlic, minced

4-inch piece fresh ginger root, peeled and finely chopped

In a large bowl, place frozen edamame. Add soy sauce, hot sauce, garlic and ginger and toss to combine. Place the edamame mixture in a microwave-safe dish, cover and return to the freezer until ready to use. When ready to serve, place the edamame mixture in the microwave on full power and cook for 8 minutes. Serve while warm.

Trivia: What is edamame? They are Japanese soybeans in their pods. Eat only the beans, not their outer covering.

Layered Taco Dip

MAKES 9 OR 10-INCH ROUND DISH OF DIP

This is an easy as well flavorful go-to recipe. Just when I think every single person I know has it, I get another recipe request. I love that it can be made ahead.

1 can (9-ounces) bean dip

1 cup light sour cream

½ cup light mayonnaise with olive oil

1 envelope (1.25-ounces) taco seasoning mix

2 ripe avocados, peeled and seeded

2 tablespoons fresh lime juice

Sea salt to taste

Freshly ground black pepper to taste

2 green onions, chopped

1 large tomatoes, seeded and chopped

½ cup black olives, chopped

½ cup finely shredded Cheddar cheese

On a 9-inch springform pan, a 10-inch glass pie plate, or 2 (5-inch) plates, using a knife, spread bean dip. In a medium bowl, combine sour cream, mayonnaise, and taco seasoning mix. Using a knife, spread the sour cream mixture over bean dip. In a small bowl, mash avocados until slightly lumpy, add lime juice and blend thoroughly. Season to taste with salt and pepper. Layer mashed avocados over the sour cream mixture. Continue to layer ingredients one at a time. Layer green onions, tomatoes, black olives and top with Cheddar cheese.

Cover and chill 4 hours or overnight for best flavors.

RECOMMENDED DIPPERS:

Taco chips

Baby carrots

Slices of zucchini

Slices of jicama

TIP: A springform pan is used for making cheesecakes. It has a spring-loaded side, is 2 to 3 inches high and opens up and separates from the bottom, making unmolding a cake very easy. This is a nice choice for this dip to show off the pretty layers. If you use a springform pan, place it on a plate larger than 10 inches and carefully remove the sides. Leaving the bottom of the pan on is fine.

Black Bean Hummus and Peaches

MAKES 12X10 INCH TRAY OR 10-INCH PIE DISH

Sweet with a little heat. Guaranteed to be a hit with your vegetarian guests.
Serve as a spread for your favorite bread or with fresh veggies for dipping.

FOR THE HUMMUS:

1 can (15-ounces) black beans, drained and rinsed

¼ cup cilantro leaves

2 tablespoons extra virgin olive oil

1 tablespoon tahini (sesame seed paste)

1 teaspoon Sriracha® sauce (found in Asian section in grocery store)

1 tablespoon lemon zest

3 tablespoons fresh lemon juice

1 clove garlic

Kosher or sea salt to taste

In a blender, place beans, cilantro, extra virgin olive oil, tahini, Sriracha® sauce, lemon zest, lemon juice, garlic and salt. Purée until well blended. Using a spatula, spread the black bean hummus on to a shallow pie dish or decorative platter. Cover with plastic wrap and chill in the refrigerator until ready to use.

FOR THE PEACH TOPPING:

1 avocado, chopped

Juice from ½ lemon

1 can (14.5-ounces) peaches in water, drained and chopped (use fresh if available)

¼ teaspoon cumin

½ teaspoon salt

In a medium bowl, place avocado. Sprinkle with lemon juice and toss gently to coat. Add peaches, cumin and salt and mix gently. Using a knife, spread the peach mixture over the top of the hummus mixture. Cover with plastic wrap and chill in the refrigerator until ready to serve.

FOR THE GARNISH:

Paprika for garnish (Smoky or Hot Spanish are preferred.)

Sprinkle lightly with paprika.

Roasted Red Pepper Hummus Platter

MAKES ONE 12 X 10-INCH PLATTER OF DIP

Hummus is a good source of protein for our vegetarian friends and just plain tastes good. Anyone can serve it in a bowl, but how pretty is this arrangement on a platter? It's all about the presentation.

FOR THE HUMMUS:

1 red bell pepper, seeded and halved

1 can (14-ounces) chick peas, drained and rinsed

¼ cup tahini

Juice of 2 lemons, about 6 tablespoons

2 tablespoons water

3 tablespoons Roasted Almond Olive Oil

or

3 tablespoons extra virgin olive oil

6 cloves garlic

1 ½ teaspoons smoky paprika

½ teaspoon ground cumin

Sea or kosher salt to taste, about ½ teaspoon

Freshly ground black pepper to taste

Preheat the broiler. Set the oven rack 4 to 6 inches from the heat source. On a baking sheet lined with aluminum foil, place pepper and broil 5 to 10 minutes, or until charred. Place in a paper bag to cool for 30 minutes and remove loose skin.

In a food processor, place pepper, chick peas, tahini, lemon juice, water, olive oil, garlic, paprika and cumin and season to taste with salt and pepper. Blend until thoroughly mixed.

TO SERVE:

Suggested vegetable dippers:

Snow peas

Carrots

Cherry tomatoes

Jicama

Asparagus

Kalamata olives, pitted

Paprika for garnish

Using a knife, spread the red pepper hummus on a bamboo cheese board or a granite or marble serving slab. Arrange dipping vegetables around the edges and sprinkle with paprika.

TIP: Hummus may be made 8 hours ahead, which allows the flavors to blend. Tahini is sesame seed paste. I like making this with rainbow carrots, which can be found at specialty food markets.

TIP: Chick peas is another name for garbanzo beans.

Hummus Roll-Ups

MAKES ABOUT 75 SPIRALS

You may also prepare this recipe for hummus and serve it in a bowl, garnished with diced sun-dried tomatoes, chopped Kalamata olives and feta cheese and served with pita bread and vegetables for dipping. Another nice garnish is chopped roasted peppers. Suddenly one recipe turns into several.

FOR THE HUMMUS:

1 can (14-ounces) chick peas

¼ cup tahini (sesame seed paste)

4 tablespoons extra virgin olive oil

Juice of 2 lemons, about 6 tablespoons

2 tablespoons water

6 garlic cloves, mashed

½ teaspoon chipotle powder or cayenne pepper

1 ½ teaspoons sweet paprika

½ teaspoon ground cumin

Sea salt to taste

¼ cup black olives

¼ cup sun-dried tomatoes

In a food processor, place chick peas, tahini, olive oil, lemon juice, water, garlic cloves, chipotle powder, paprika, cumin and salt and process until fairly smooth. Add black olives and sundried tomatoes and pulse until just chopped.

TO MAKE THE ROLL UPS:

1 package (20-ounces) tortillas, plain or flavored, corn or flour, 8-count, large, burrito-sized

Using a knife, spread a thin layer of hummus on 1 tortilla. Beginning at one end and rolling to the other, tightly roll tortilla. Wrap tightly in plastic wrap and refrigerate until ready to use. When ready to serve, using a sharp knife, slice into ½-inch spirals.

TIP: You may make this ahead and freeze it until ready to use. When ready to serve, thaw for 30 minutes and slice with a sharp knife into spirals about ½ inch.

Guacamole

MAKES 1 MEDIUM-SIZED BOWL OF DIP

Did you know that avocados are actually fruit? They are also an excellent source of Vitamin E, antioxidants, contain healthy fat and more potassium than bananas. So enjoy this guacamole guilt-free.

2 ripe avocados, peeled and pitted

2 large tomatoes, seeded and chopped

¼ cup sweet onion, chopped

1 jalapeño, seeded and chopped

2 garlic cloves, minced

¼ cup fresh cilantro, chopped

Juice of 2 limes

Ground cumin to taste

Sea salt to taste

Freshly ground black pepper to taste

Lime slices for prepping and garnishing the bowl

Margarita salt for garnishing the bowl

Vegetable dippers

Taco chips

In a medium bowl, combine avocados, tomatoes, onion, jalapeño, garlic, cilantro, lime juice, cumin, salt and pepper. Mix until well blended but still chunky. Taste and adjust seasonings.

To serve: Dampen the rim of a giant margarita glass with a wedge of lime. On a flat plate, arrange margarita or kosher salt in a circle about the size of the rim of the glass. Dip the glass into kosher or margarita salt. It should resemble the salt around a margarita. Spoon dip into the glass and place a slice of lime on the edge. Serve with veggie dippers and chips.

TIP: If not serving immediately, wait to salt the edge of the glass until just before serving. To help retard browning, place dip in an airtight container.

Vegetable Spring Rolls

MAKES 15

Light and refreshing, this Asian inspired appetizer is a keeper.

12-ounces baby carrots, cut julienne style

6 green onions, cut julienne style

1 red pepper, cut julienne style

5 radishes, sliced thinly

1/8 head cabbage, shredded

1 package (22-ounces) 9-inch rice paper (found in Asian grocery stores)

Set prepared vegetables aside. In a large frying pan, heat one-inch of water to warm, not hot. Keep the water warm but do not allow to boil. Place one piece of rice paper in the water and allow to soften up for one minute. Carefully remove rice paper from water and place flat on a large work surface such as a cutting board.

1 bunch cilantro, leaves separated from stems

Hoisin sauce

Sriracha® Chile Sauce

Drizzle one teaspoon of hoisin sauce over entire piece of cooked rice paper. Place a thin layer of carrots, green onions, red pepper, radishes and cabbage over hoisin sauce. Slowly roll rice paper up gently and tightly. Just before sealing the end, take 3 cilantro leaves and place on what will be the outermost layer. Continue rolling. Seal edges of spring roll with wet fingers. The cilantro makes a nice garnish as it will show through the paper. Serve on small plate with Sriracha® drizzled beneath.

TIP: If any guests are not fans of cilantro, leave it out of a few spring rolls.

Beef, Chicken & Pork

Spicy Beef and Peach Kabobs

Tenderloin Sliders with
Caramelized Onions

Artichoke Bottoms with Blue
Cheese, Apple and Bacon

Dry Coffee Rub for Steak

Spicy Chicken Saté
with Peanut Sauce

Bacon and Pineapple Kabobs

Chicken Yakitori Kabobs

Phyllo-Wrapped Chicken
with Poblano Pesto

Stuffed Jalapeños

Pasta and Prosciutto Spirals
with Béchamel Sauce

Prosciutto-Wrapped
Cantaloupe

Pork Tenderloin Kabobs
with Ginger Sauce

Pork Egg Rolls with Sweet
and Sour Sauce

Caramelized Bacon-
Wrapped Avocado

Prosciutto-Wrapped Asparagus

Spicy Beef and Peach Kabobs

SERVES ABOUT 10

This one hits it out of the park—sweet peaches, steak and just a hint of heat from the chipotle. And, it is really simple to prepare.

5 tablespoons peach preserves

1 chipotle chile in adobo sauce, chopped

1 ½ pounds rib-eye, skirt, or top sirloin steak

Seasoned salt to taste

Freshly ground black pepper to taste

1 can (24-ounces) sliced peaches in water, drained

Cooking spray for prepping grill

Presoak 6-inch wooden skewers for at least two hours. In a small bowl, combine preserves and chipotle. Set aside.

Spray the grill with non-stick spray. Preheat the grill to high. Using a sharp knife, cut beef into 1-inch cubes. Season to taste with seasoned salt and pepper. Thread 2 beef cubes and 2 peach slices onto presoaked 6-inch wooden skewers. Repeat until all ingredients have been used.

Grill kabobs over a high heat about 3 to 4 minutes per side, turning once. Remove skewers from the grill. Using a basting brush, brush kabobs generously with the peach preserves mixture.

TO SERVE:

1 ½ cups prepared mango salsa

¼ cup fresh cilantro, chopped

In a small decorative bowl, combine mango salsa and cilantro. Serve on the side as a condiment for the kabobs.

TIP: *Why soak the wooden skewers in advance? This keeps them from burning up while on the grill. Chipotle chiles in adobo sauce come in a can and are found in the Latin section of the supermarket.*

TIP: *What exactly is a chipotle pepper? It is a smoked jalapeño.*

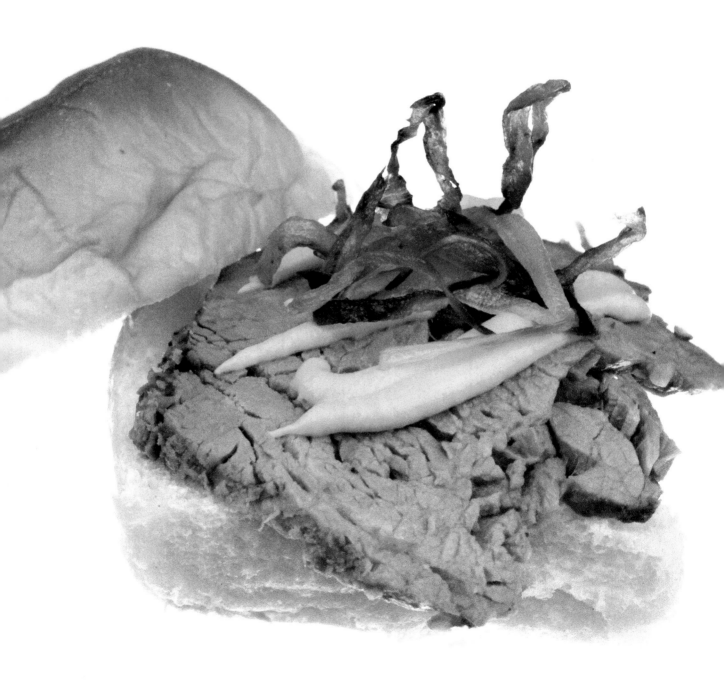

Tenderloin Sliders with Caramelized Onions

MAKES ABOUT 40 SLIDERS

This recipe is a crowd-pleaser and a big hit with kids. I served this at one of many graduation parties and overheard one high school boy telling another, "They have beef tenderloin at this party." After serving it many times, I have found it to be the protein of choice for any large gathering.

FOR THE TENDERLOIN:

5 pounds beef tenderloin, trimmed

1 bottle (15-ounces) lite soy sauce

1 cup Italian flavored bread crumbs

1 tablespoon garlic powder

1 tablespoon McCormick® seasoned pepper, regular or hot

In a large bowl, place beef and pour entire bottle of soy sauce over beef. Cover and marinate beef in the refrigerator for 2 hours, turning occasionally. In a medium bowl, combine bread crumbs, garlic powder and seasoned pepper. On a flat surface, like a cutting board, spread the seasoning mixture. Remove beef from the marinade and discard the marinade. Roll beef in the seasoning mixture, coating all sides.

Preheat the oven to 500 degrees. Fold beef in half lengthwise and tie beef together tightly with butcher's string or dental floss. Roast at 500 degrees for 15 minutes, then reduce heat to 350 degrees and continue roasting for 1 hour for medium rare. Cool. Using a sharp knife, thinly slice beef.

FOR THE ONIONS:

1 teaspoon butter

1 medium, sweet onion, thinly sliced and chopped

½ teaspoon granulated sugar

Dash of salt, optional (less than 1/8 teaspoon)

½ teaspoon butter

½ teaspoon balsamic vinegar

Tenderloin Sliders continued

Place a medium, heavy skillet over medium-high heat. Add 1 teaspoon butter and onion and sauté 10 minutes, stirring occasionally. Onion should brown but not burn. Add sugar and salt, lower the heat to medium-low, and sauté another 10 minutes, stirring occasionally. Add ½ teaspoon butter and sauté 10 more minutes, for a total of 30 minutes. Turn the heat off and add balsamic vinegar, stirring to combine.

TO SERVE:

Sliced tenderloin, at room temperature

40 small slider buns

Caramelized onions

Horseradish

Mustard

Mayonnaise

Place sliced tenderloin on sliders buns and top with caramelized onions. Serve with horseradish, mustard and mayonnaise.

Artichoke Bottoms

SERVES 6-8

Artichoke bottoms may be found online and in specialty health food stores in the canned vegetable section. They make a great platform on which to build interesting appetizers.

Be creative! For a vegetarian version, substitute sun-dried tomatoes for the bacon.

¼ tart apple, cored and chopped into small cubes (a variety is suggested)

¼ cup blue cheese

1 can (14-ounces) artichoke bottoms, drained and rinsed (6 to 8 per can)

1 slice bacon, fried crisp and cut into 1-inch pieces (or 6-8 pieces of sun-dried tomatoes)

Preheat the oven to 350 degrees. If necessary, flip artichoke bottoms over and slice off the bottom so the bottoms are flat and sit level. Reserve any pieces you remove for your next salad. Place bottoms in an ungreased, oven-proof dish, open side up.

In a small bowl, place apples and blue cheese and toss gently to combine. Fill artichoke bottoms with the apple mixture. Tuck 1 piece of bacon into the center of each artichoke. Bake for 10 minutes, or until cheese is melted. Serve hot.

Dry Coffee Rub for Steak

4 VERY GENEROUS SERVINGS OR 8 SMALL PLATES

This rub is fantastic but be sure to complete the experience with the espresso vinegar. It can be found at specialty olive oil and vinegar shops and is worth the search!

4 pounds rib eye steak

1/3 cup coffee grounds (regular caffeinated coffee beans that are ground)

2 teaspoons garlic powder

2 teaspoons paprika

1 tablespoon brown sugar

1 tablespoon salt

1 teaspoon freshly ground black pepper

½ cup Espresso Balsamic Vinegar

Remove steaks from the refrigerator and bring to room temperature about 1 hour before grilling. This helps prevent the steaks from sticking to the grill.

In a small bowl, combine the coffee, garlic powder, paprika, brown sugar, salt and pepper. Press the dry rub into steaks on all sides. Let the dry rub sit at least 30 minutes before grilling. If not using within the hour, place back in refrigerator and bring to room temperature before cooking.

Preheat the grill to a hot heat, 500 degrees. Grill steaks over hot coals about 8 minutes, or until cooked to the desired doneness, about 4 minutes per side for charred rare.

While steaks are grilling, in a small saucepan, place vinegar over low heat and cook 5 minutes or until vinegar is reduced/thick and syrupy. Remove from heat and cover until needed. Drizzle vinegar while warm over steaks.

Spicy Chicken Saté with Peanut Sauce

SERVES 20

If you've never made peanut sauce, that needs to change.
It is easy and so delicious you will never buy it again.

TO MARINATE CHICKEN:

4 pounds boneless, skinless chicken breasts

2 cups canned unsweetened, lite coconut milk

4 teaspoons turmeric

1 teaspoon salt

Using a sharp knife, cut chicken breasts into 4-inch long, ½-inch wide strips. In a large bowl, combine coconut milk, turmeric and salt. Add chicken, tossing to coat. Cover and refrigerate 1 to 8 hours.

FOR THE SAUCE: (Makes 1 cup)

1/2 cup creamy peanut butter

1/3 cup canned unsweetened, lite coconut milk

1 serrano or jalapeño pepper, seeded and minced

2 green onions, minced

¼ cup fresh cilantro, chopped

3 tablespoons fresh lemon or lime juice

2 tablespoons fish sauce or low-sodium soy sauce

1/2-inch piece fresh ginger root, peeled and minced

1 clove garlic, minced

1 teaspoon sugar or to taste

In a blender or food processor, combine peanut butter, coconut milk, serrano pepper, green onions, cilantro, lemon juice, fish sauce, ginger, garlic and sugar and process until smooth. Cover and refrigerate until ready to serve.

TO ASSEMBLE CHICKEN SATÉ: Preheat the grill to high or preheat the broiler. Drain chicken and discard marinade. Thread 2 to 3 pieces of chicken onto 1 (6-inch) skewer ribbon-style. Bring the chicken to room temperature. Grill over a hot grate about 2 to 3 minutes per side, or until grill marks appear on chicken. If broiling, position rack 5 inches from the heating element and broil 2 to 3 minutes per side, or until chicken is cooked through. Using a paring knife, cut into meat to be sure it is cooked through before serving.

Spicy Chicken Saté continued

TO SERVE:

Cooked chicken skewers

Prepared rice

Prepared couscous

Shredded zucchini

Shredded carrots

Peanut sauce

Lime slices for garnish

Cilantro leaves for garnish

Place chicken skewers over rice, couscous or shredded zucchini and carrots as shown in the picture. Drizzle the peanut sauce over the chicken skewers and garnish with lime and or cilantro leaves. Serve extra peanut sauce on the side.

TIP: This recipe for peanut sauce can be made in advance. Coconut milk and fish sauce can be found in the Asian section of your supermarket.

Bacon and Pineapple Kabobs

MAKES 40

Sweet and salty—this one has it all!

1/3 cup brown sugar

1/2 teaspoon chipotle powder

1/2 teaspoon ground cinnamon

1/2 teaspoon freshly ground black pepper

2 packages (2.52-ounces) microwave-ready bacon, cut in half crosswise

1 can (20-ounces) pineapple chunks, drained

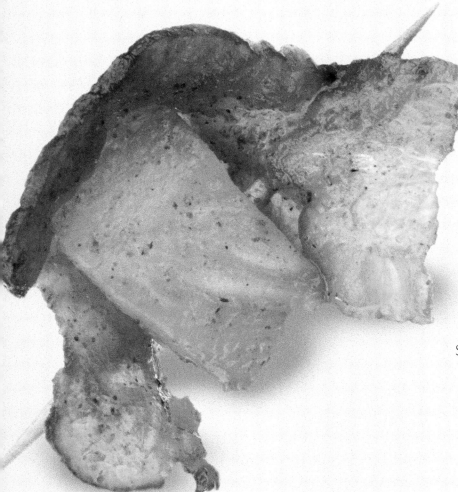

Preheat the oven to 400 degrees. In a flat dish like a pie plate, combine brown sugar, chipotle powder, cinnamon and black pepper. Dredge bacon halves in the brown sugar mixture, coating both sides well.

Place a pineapple chunk on one end of bacon halve and roll up, securing with a toothpick. Continue until all ingredients are used.

Place skewers on a broiler pan so juices will drip down, allowing bacon to crisp. Bake for 6 minutes. Serve hot.

Chicken Yakitori Kabobs

MAKES ABOUT 10 KABOBS

This recipe is a huge hit every time I serve it.

2 pounds boneless, skinless chicken breasts, uncooked

1 cup low-sodium soy sauce

¼ cup sesame oil

¼ cup fresh lemon juice

¼ cup sugar

4 green onions, thinly sliced

2 tablespoons sesame seeds

2 garlic cloves, minced

2 teaspoons fresh ginger, minced

1 red bell pepper, cut into 1-inch cubes

½ cup uncooked basmati rice

Using a sharp knife, cube chicken into 1-inch squares. In a large bowl, combine soy sauce, sesame oil, lemon juice, sugar, green onions, sesame seeds, garlic and ginger. Add chicken to the marinade and toss to coat. Cover and marinate in the refrigerator for 8 hours, or overnight.

Preheat the grill to 400 degrees or high. Remove chicken from the marinade and discard marinade. Thread 2 pieces chicken onto 6-inch skewers. Thread 1-piece pepper, chicken, pepper. Thread 2 more pieces chicken onto skewer. Repeat this skewer sequence with remaining ingredients.

Prepare basmati rice according to package directions.

Grill skewers for 4 minutes per side, or until done, turning frequently. Using small plates, serve kabobs over rice.

Phyllo-Wrapped Chicken with Poblano Pesto

SERVES 4 LUCKY PEOPLE

Spice up your entertaining with flavorful chicken bundles. Buttery phyllo, moist chicken and spirited pesto is a treat to the taste buds.

FOR THE PESTO:

1 poblano (pasilla) pepper

¼ cup fresh spinach leaves

1/8 cup grated Romano cheese

2 tablespoons pine nuts, toasted

1 tablespoon chipotle sauce

1 clove garlic

¼ cup extra virgin olive oil

Sea salt to taste

Freshly ground black pepper to taste

Preheat the oven to 500 degrees. On a baking sheet, place pepper and roast in the oven for 30 minutes, or until skins are completely wrinkled and charred, turning twice during roasting. In a bowl, place pepper, cover and cool for 30 minutes. Peel off loose skin, seed and core. In a food processor, place roasted pepper, spinach, Romano cheese, pine nuts, chipotle sauce and garlic and process until blended. While processing, slowly pour in olive oil. Season to taste with salt and pepper. Set pesto aside.

TO ASSEMBLE BUNDLES:

4 pieces phyllo dough, thawed in the refrigerator according to package directions

4 tablespoons butter, melted

8 ounces cooked, boneless, skinless chicken breasts, cut into 4 (2-ounce) pieces

Freshly ground black pepper to taste

½ cup white Cheddar cheese, shredded

Reserved poblano pesto

8 pieces fresh chives

Spinach leaves for garnish

Preheat the oven to 400 degrees. On a flat surface, unroll 1-piece phyllo dough. Using a pastry brush, brush dough with melted butter. Fold dough in half like a book and butter again. Place a piece of chicken in the center of dough. Season to taste with pepper. Place 1 tablespoon of the pesto on top of chicken and 1 tablespoon shredded cheese on top of the pesto. Carefully fold up bottom to cover chicken, then fold top down over bottom. Fold sides of dough over the top and bottom pieces. Butter phyllo seams to seal. Place chicken bundles, seam side down, in an ungreased ovenproof dish. Repeat with remaining chicken. Do not cover. Bake for 25 minutes, or until lightly golden.

Place 2 pieces of chives over top of chicken like an "X". Line a decorative plate with spinach greens and serve chicken bundles hot over greens.

Stuffed Jalapeños

MAKES AT LEAST 20 PEPPER HALVES

10 jalapeño peppers

Cooking spray for prepping baking sheet

¾ package (6-ounces) cream cheese, room temperature

½ teaspoon seasoned salt

¼ teaspoon freshly ground black pepper

2 slices preservative-free, nitrate and nitrite-free bacon, cooked

Preheat the broiler. Using a sharp knife, slice peppers in half lengthwise and remove stem and seeds. On a sprayed baking sheet, place peppers cut-side down and broil for 5 minutes. Cool on the baking sheet.

Lower the oven temperature to 350 degrees.

In a small bowl, combine cream cheese, salt and pepper. Using a spoon, fill the pepper cavities with the cream cheese mixture. If peppers are quite large, cut the halves in half lengthwise after stuffing. Using a sharp knife, slice 1 small strip

bacon for each jalapeño halve, about 1 inch by ¼ inch. Place bacon strip over the cheese mixture, gently pressing down to secure. Bake the stuffed peppers for 10 minutes, or until hot. Serve hot.

TIP: Wear gloves or use a knife and fork when handling hot peppers and removing their seeds to avoid getting pepper juice on your fingertips, especially if you wear contact lenses.

Trivia: Dried jalapeños are known as chipotles.

Pasta and Prosciutto with Béchamel Sauce

SERVES 10

I was inspired to create this tasty appetizer after eating something similar in an Italian restaurant in the Memphis area. It is a keeper.

5 lasagna noodles, uncooked

Fill a large kettle with water and place over high heat. When water is boiling, add lasagna noodles and cook al dente, about 8 minutes according to package directions. Drain.

FOR THE BÉCHAMEL SAUCE:

2 tablespoons butter

1 tablespoon all-purpose flour

1/4 teaspoon sea or kosher salt

1/8 teaspoon white pepper

1/2 cup half-and-half

1/2 cup low-sodium chicken broth

1 tablespoon grated white onion

Dash dried thyme leaves, less than 1/8 teaspoon

Dash cayenne pepper, less than 1/8 teaspoon

In a small saucepan, place butter and melt over medium heat. Add flour, salt and white pepper and whisk briskly so lumps do not form.

Slowly add half-and-half and chicken broth, whisking continually so lumps do not form. Add onion, thyme and cayenne pepper and continue stirring until sauce thickens. Remove the saucepan from the heat, cover and set aside.

TO ASSEMBLE SPIRALS:

Cooked lasagna noodles

1/4 cup mascarpone cheese

1 package (3 ounces) prosciutto, sliced

Béchamel sauce

Pasta and Prosciutto continued

Preheat the oven to 325 degrees.

On a flat surface, lay out cooked lasagna noodles. Using a knife, spread mascarpone cheese evenly over each noodle. Place 1-piece prosciutto over cheese, trimming prosciutto if necessary. Prosciutto should cover length of noodle but not extend over the sides.

Roll noodles up tightly from the narrow end and secure with two toothpicks. Cut the roll in half, creating two spirals. Place spirals cut side down in an ungreased baking dish. Drizzle half of the béchamel sauce over tops of spirals. Keep reserved sauce warm. Bake for 15 minutes until sauce browns slightly.

TO SERVE:
Spinach leaves for plating

Reserved béchamel sauce
Paprika for garnishing

Using 10 small plates, line plates with spinach leaves. Carefully remove toothpicks from spirals and place 1 spiral, scallop-side of noodle up, on each plate. Spoon excess béchamel sauce over each spiral. Sprinkle tops of noodles with paprika. Serve warm.

TIP: I have never found a pasta dish I didn't like. This one is no exception. I love the lasagna's texture combined with the creamy cheese and salty prosciutto. This recipe is really easy and will impress your guests. Make the spirals ahead and drizzle the béchamel sauce on just before baking.

Prosciutto-Wrapped Cantaloupe

MAKES ABOUT 32

Sweet, salty and refreshing.

1 ripe cantaloupe, sliced in half and seeded

1 package (3-ounces)

prosciutto, cut into 1-inch by 4-inch strips

32 fresh basil leaves

Using a melon baller, scoop cantaloupe into 1-inch balls. On a flat surface like a cutting board, lay 1 prosciutto slice. Place 1 melon ball in the center of the slice, fold both ends of prosciutto up and over ball. Place a basil leaf on top of prosciutto and firmly secure with a toothpick. Repeat until all ingredients have been used. Cover and chill. Serve on a decorative plate.

TIP: This recipe needs to be made the same day as it is served. You may have some cantaloupe balls leftover. If so, put them in an air-tight container, refrigerate, and eat them later.

Pork Tenderloin Kabobs with Ginger Sauce

MAKES 12 TO 18 SMALL KABOBS

FOR THE PORK MARINADE:

1 ¼ pounds pork tenderloin

6 green onions, sliced

1 jalapeño pepper, chopped

3 tablespoons extra virgin olive oil

1 tablespoon sesame oil

1 tablespoon fresh lime juice

2 large cloves garlic, chopped

1-inch piece fresh ginger, peeled and grated

Using a sharp knife, cut pork into 1-inch cubes. In a small bowl, combine green onions, jalapeño, olive oil, sesame oil, lime juice, garlic and ginger. In a large Ziploc bag, place pork and marinade. Seal bag and toss several times to coat pork. Refrigerate for 4 to 6 hours, turning bag occasionally.

FOR THE GINGER SAUCE:

1 tablespoon coconut oil

½ cup red onion, chopped

2-inch piece fresh ginger, peeled and grated

1 clove garlic, chopped

1 can (14.5-ounces) diced tomatoes with juices

¼ cup rice vinegar

3 tablespoons low-sodium soy sauce

1 tablespoon sugar

1/8 teaspoon crushed red pepper flakes

In a medium saucepan, place coconut oil over medium heat and sauté onion until tender, about 5 minutes. Add ginger and garlic and sauté for 1 more minute. Add diced tomatoes and juices, rice vinegar, soy sauce, sugar and red pepper flakes and stir to combine. Reduce heat to low and simmer sauce uncovered for 10 minutes, stirring occasionally. Into a blender, pour sauce and purée until smooth. Return the sauce to the saucepan and keep warm over a low heat.

TO COOK KABOBS:

Marinated pork cubes

Cooking spray for grill

Remove pork cubes from the marinade and discard marinade. Thread pork cubes onto 4 to 6-inch wooden skewers. Spray the grill with nonstick cooking spray and preheat the grill to high. Place kabobs on grate and cook about 3 minutes per side, or until meat is no longer pink. Serve over rice with ginger sauce on the side.

TIP: Rice vinegar is normally found in the Asian section of the supermarket.

Pork Egg Rolls with Sweet and Sour Sauce

SERVES 20 PEOPLE 2 EGGROLLS EACH

I rarely fry anything, but I make an exception with egg rolls. This recipe is mouth-watering. Add an Asian influence to your next party with this delicious recipe.

FOR THE FILLING:

1 pound ground pork sausage

1 can (8-ounces) bamboo shoots, drained and chopped

1 can (8-ounces) water chestnuts, drained and diced

6 ounces mushrooms, cleaned and diced

4 cups shredded cabbage

1/2 red bell pepper, seeded and chopped

4 green onions, chopped

1 large clove garlic, minced

1 inch fresh ginger root, peeled and diced

Freshly ground black pepper, to taste

3 tablespoons lite soy sauce

1 tablespoon black bean sauce with garlic

½ teaspoon sugar

1 teaspoon Chinese five-spice powder

1 teaspoon cornstarch

In a large skillet, brown sausage over a medium heat, crumbling it with a fork, until sausage is cooked through and no longer pink. Using a slotted spoon, remove cooked sausage and place on paper towels to drain, reserving pan drippings.

To the same skillet, add bamboo shoots, water chestnuts, mushrooms, cabbage, pepper, green onions, garlic and ginger and cook until vegetables are limp. Season to taste with pepper.

In a small bowl, place soy sauce, black bean sauce, sugar, Chinese five-spice and cornstarch and stir until blended well. Add the soy sauce mixture to the vegetable mixture and stir to combine. Return cooked sausage to the skillet and heat for 1 minute, stirring to combine. Set aside.

Pork Egg Rolls continued

TO ASSEMBLE EGG ROLLS:
2 packages (16-ounces) egg roll wrappers

Peanut oil for frying

Unwrap egg roll wrappers and cover with moist paper towels to keep from drying out. On a flat surface like a cutting board, lay 1 wrap with a corner pointed towards you. Using a spoon, place a heaping teaspoon of the pork mixture in the center of the wrap. With damp fingers, fold the bottom of the wrap up over the pork mixture. Fold both sides of the wrap over the bottom. Roll the bottom up toward the top, sealing the top corner over the bundle like an envelope. Using your fingers, moisten the roll with water to seal. Transfer roll, seam side down, to a paper towel lined baking sheet and cover loosely with damp paper towels. Continue to make egg rolls, transferring to the baking sheet and covering with paper towels as formed until all ingredients are used.

Fill a medium skillet with 1 inch of peanut oil and place over medium-high heat until the oil reaches 350 degrees. Add 5 egg rolls at a time and cook for about 3 minutes per side. Oil should be hot enough to brown the egg rolls. Using a slotted spoon, transfer cooked egg rolls from the skillet to a cooling rack lined with several layers of paper towels to drain. Fry remaining egg rolls in batches, transferring to the cooling rack.

Preheat the oven to 250 degrees. Position the oven rack in the middle of the oven. Transfer egg rolls to a baking sheet and keep warm until ready to serve.

FOR THE SWEET AND SOUR SAUCE:
¼ cup sweet chile sauce

¼ cup black raspberry fruit spread

In a small saucepan, place chile sauce and fruit spread over a medium heat and continue stirring until combined. Serve warm on the side.

TIP: Egg roll wrappers are normally found in your supermarket in the refrigerated section of the produce department. If you can't find black raspberry fruit spread, you can substitute it with grape or plum spread.

Caramelized Bacon-Wrapped Avocado

MAKES 8 PIECES

Bacon lovers adore this one. Creamy avocado wrapped up in salty spicy bacon—delicious!!

½ cup brown sugar

1/8 teaspoon cumin

1/8 teaspoon cayenne pepper

2 tablespoon maple syrup

1 ripe but firm avocado

4 pieces of thin, uncooked bacon, sliced in half lengthwise

Preheat oven to 375 degrees. In a flat dish such as a pie plate, combine brown sugar, cumin, cayenne and maple syrup. Dredge bacon halves in maple syrup mixture, coating both sides well.

Using a sharp knife, cut avocado in half lengthwise. Separate halves and remove seed. Carefully remove skin from each half, then cut each half into 4 long strips.

Wrap a piece of bacon carefully around each slice of avocado and place on broiler pan so that juices will be allowed to drip down, allowing bacon to crisp. Bake for 25 minutes, cool slightly before serving.

TIP: The bacon is supple enough that it wraps easily around the avocado and thus does not need a toothpick to hold it in place.

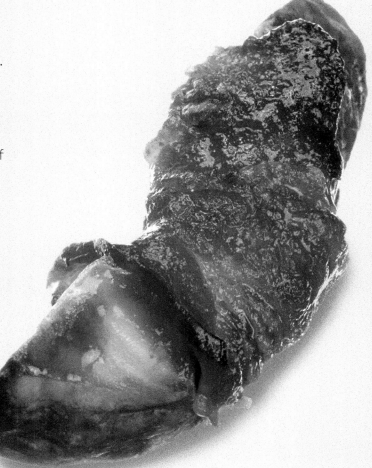

Prosciutto-Wrapped Asparagus

MAKES ABOUT 8 TO 10 BUNDLES

This is a tasty dish, and it can be made in advance.
Don't skimp on the zest as it makes all the flavors pop.

2 bunches fresh asparagus, about 2 pounds

¼ cup water

4 ounces mascarpone cheese, room temperature

or

1/2 package (4-ounces) cream cheese, softened

2 tablespoons fresh basil leaves, chopped

2 tablespoons pine nuts, toasted and chopped

1 tablespoon water

1 tablespoon orange zest

2 packages (3-ounces) prosciutto, cut into 4 inch strips

Freshly ground black pepper

Using a sharp knife, cut tough ends from asparagus. Place asparagus in a microwave-safe dish. Add water and cover loosely. Cook on high for 4 minutes, or until asparagus is bright green and tender. Rinse asparagus under cold water, drain and set aside.

In a small bowl, combine mascarpone cheese, fresh basil, pine nuts, water and orange zest. Season to taste with pepper.

On a flat surface like a cutting board, lay 2 prosciutto strips at a time. Using a knife, spread 1 teaspoon of the cheese mixture over the length of the meat. Position 2 stalks of asparagus at one end so that the prosciutto is at the base of the asparagus and carefully roll up. Press the end of prosciutto to seal. Repeat steps until all ingredients are used. Refrigerate until needed. Serve at room temperature.

TIP: Toasting pine nuts is just like toasting other nuts. Place nuts in small frying pan, heat on medium heat and turn often to brown.

TIP: This small plate may be made the day before it is needed to save time.

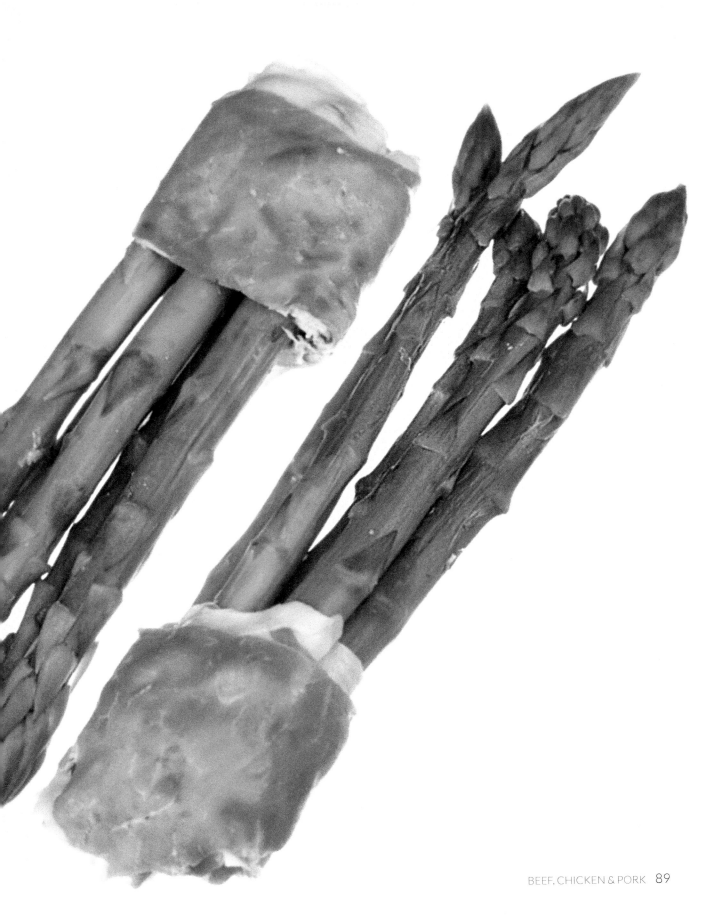

Seafood

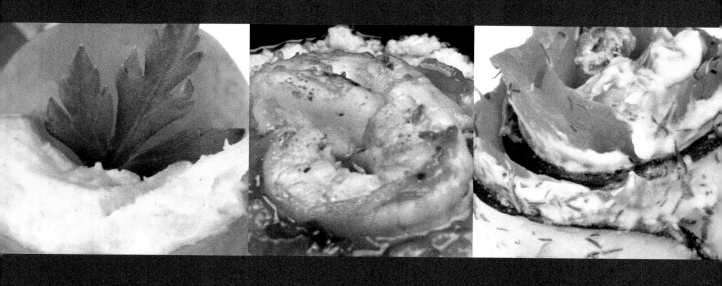

Grilled Coconut Shrimp

Crab Stuffed Cherry Tomatoes

Shrimp and Grits Southern Style

Mango Gazpacho with
Blackened Shrimp

Langostino and Pesto in
Mini Phyllo Cups

Grilled Avocado with Shrimp

Squash and Salmon Roll-Ups

Hot Crabster Brie Dip

Mustard and Herb
Encrusted Salmon

Sautéed Calamari with Roasted
Tomato Salsa and Lemon

Stuffed and Grilled Squid

Spaghetti Squash and Scallops

Roasted Peach Soup
with Scallops

Grilled Coconut Shrimp

MAKES 10 TO 15 APPETIZER KABOBS

Don't be frightened by the coconut balsamic and lime olive oil.
They are easy to find in specialty olive oil and vinegar shops.

¼ cup coconut balsamic vinegar

¼ cup lime olive oil

Zest of 1 lime

1 pound large (31 to 35 per pound) wild shrimp, peeled, deveined and tails removed

Freshly ground black pepper to taste

Shredded coconut, unsweetened

Preheat the grill to 350 degrees. In a large bowl, combine vinegar, olive oil and zest. Add shrimp and marinate in the refrigerator for at least 1 hour. Remove shrimp from the marinade and discard marinade. Using 4-inch long wooden skewers, slide 3 shrimp onto each skewer. Season shrimp to taste with pepper, then dredge in coconut. Grill about 2 minutes per side, or until shrimp are pink. Serve warm.

TIP: Having the tails removed makes this so much easier to eat at a cocktail party. I once was faced with a glass of wine in one hand and a plate of shrimp in the other with no surface to set either down. Well, that tail was a challenge I will never put my guests through.

Crab-Stuffed Cherry Tomatoes

SERVES 25 WITH 2 TOMATOES PER PERSON

This recipe can be made a day in advance and refrigerated, which allows the flavors to blend.

50 cherry tomatoes

4 tablespoons butter, softened

1 package (8-ounces) cream cheese, softened

4 tablespoons light mayonnaise

Juice of 1 large lemon (about 3 tablespoons)

2 teaspoons Old Bay Seafood Seasoning®

10 ounces cooked crab, shredded (use canned only if desperate)

Reserved tomato tops for garnish

Parsley leaves for garnish

Set the tomatoes on a flat surface until they do not roll or move. That is the position they will be in later. Using a serrated knife, cut the top third off each tomato, reserving the tops for garnish. Using a small spoon, scoop out seeds. Drain each tomato by inverting it on paper towels until any extra moisture is gone.

In a medium bowl, combine butter, cream cheese, mayonnaise, onion, lemon juice, Old Bay® and crab. Mix until well blended.

Fill a quart-sized baggie with the crab mixture. Seal shut. With kitchen shears, cut off one bottom corner creating a hole large enough to squeeze mixture out. Fill each tomato with the crab mixture by gently squeezing baggie. Garnish with reserved tomato tops and parsley. Chill for four hours, then serve.

Shrimp and Grits Southern Style

SERVES 4

True Southern cooking includes grits. I was inspired to create this dish while attending a wedding rehearsal dinner in Memphis, Tennessee. I love both its presentation in cast iron skillets as well as its explosion of flavors.

1 serving cooked grits

1 tablespoon butter

½ teaspoon garlic powder

Cooking spray

Preheat the oven to 300 degrees and preheat the grill to a medium-high heat. In a medium saucepan, prepare grits according to package directions. Add butter and garlic powder, stir to combine, cover and keep warm. Spray the bottoms of 4 (5-inch) cast iron skillets with cooking spray. Using a spoon, place a layer of grits in each skillet, dividing grits equally between skillets. Place skillets in the oven to keep warm.

8 large (31 to 35 per pound) shrimp, peeled, deveined and tails removed

Extra virgin olive oil for brushing

Smoky paprika to taste

Using a basting brush, brush shrimp with olive oil. Season shrimp to taste with paprika. Thread shrimp on to a skewer and grill about 2 minutes per side, or until pink. Remove from the grill and keep warm.

8 tablespoons Pineapple, Serrano, Honey, Balsamic & Lime Marmalade

1 teaspoon chipotle in adobo sauce, chopped

or

8 tablespoons Robert Rothschild Roasted Pineapple Habanero Sauce

1 teaspoon chipotle in adobo sauce, chopped

In a small, microwave-safe bowl, combine marmalade and chipotle. Cover and place in the microwave and cook on high for 30 seconds.

Remove the skillets from the oven. Using a knife, spread ¼ of the marmalade mixture over top of each skillet of grits. Place 2 shrimp in the center of each skillet on top of marmalade. Place skillets on small plates to serve.

TIP: Due to the seasonality of some ingredients, flexibility may be necessary when selecting the marmalade flavor. The important thing is to use a flavor of jam or marmalade that has a lemon or lime base. The chipotle should always be added for a little kick. I love to experiment.

Mango Gazpacho with Blackened Shrimp

MAKES 2 QUARTS SOUP

Sweet, salty and spicy....a delight for the taste buds.
Save time by making this soup the day before.

FOR THE SOUP:

3 fresh mangoes, peeled and seeded

1 apple, peeled and cored

1 cucumber, peeled and seeded

4 ounces carrots, peeled, tops removed

1 jalapeño, seeded

1 can (11-ounces) coconut water

Juice of 1 lime, about 2 tablespoons

Zest of ½ orange, about 1 ½ tablespoons

3-inches fresh ginger, minced

1 teaspoon ground cumin

Sea salt to taste

Freshly ground black pepper to taste

In a blender, place mangoes, apple, cucumber, carrots, jalapeño, coconut water, lime juice, orange zest, ginger, cumin, salt and pepper and whirl until thoroughly blended. Cover and chill in the refrigerator until ready to use. Make a day in advance to allow the flavors to meld.

FOR THE SHRIMP:

3 tablespoons dried oregano leaves

3 tablespoons dried thyme leaves

1 teaspoon dried parsley leaves

3 ½ tablespoons smoky paprika

½ teaspoon cayenne pepper

2 tablespoons garlic powder

3 ½ tablespoons onion powder

1 ¾ tablespoons kosher or sea salt

3 tablespoons freshly ground black pepper

1 ¾ tablespoons white pepper

In a mortar, place oregano, thyme, parsley, paprika, cayenne, garlic powder, onion powder, salt and black and white pepper. Using the pestle, grind spices into a fine powder. Mix well. Store in an airtight glass jar.

Mango Gazpacho continued

1 pound large (31-35 per pound) wild shrimp, peeled, deveined, tail removed

1 bunch fresh cilantro leaves

Cooking spray

In a large bowl, place shrimp and sprinkle generously with the blackening spice mixture and toss until well coated. You will not need all the blackening spice mixture. Spray a large skillet with cooking spray and place over a high heat. Add shrimp to the skillet and sauté for 1 to 2 minutes a side, or until shrimp are pink. Take care not to overcook, which gives shrimp a rubbery texture. Serve immediately or cover and chill in the refrigerator until ready to serve with gazpacho.

When ready to serve, into 2, 4 or 6-ounce shot glasses pour soup. Garnish by hanging 1 shrimp on the rim and floating a sprig of cilantro in the middle.

Langostino and Pesto in Mini Phyllo Cups

MAKES 15 APPETIZERS

Langostinos are edible crustaceans, which resemble small lobsters or large shrimp. If you can't find langostinos, substitute shrimp or lobster. This recipe serves 15 if your guests only eat one....good luck with that!

15 mini phyllo shells

5 tablespoons prepared basil pesto (or fresh pesto found on page 15)

15 pieces cooked langostino, thawed (use shrimp if langostino is not available)

Old Bay® Seafood Seasoning, to taste

Zest from 1 lemon

Preheat the oven to 350 degrees.

In an ovenproof dish, place mini phyllo shells. Using a spoon, place a teaspoonful of basil pesto in each shell.

Arrange a piece of langostino on top of pesto. Season to taste with Old Bay® Seafood Seasoning. Arrange a couple pieces of zest on the top of langostino. Bake about 10 minutes, or until phyllo shells are lightly golden. Serve warm.

TIP: Never heat or reheat the phyllo shells in the microwave as they will become chewy and mushy. Heating in the oven keeps them nice and crispy. There are infinite uses for these little treasures so have fun with them!

TIP: Mini phyllo shells are refrigerated and ready to be used.

Grilled Avocado with Shrimp

SERVES 8

The oil and salt create a nice, crunchy layer on top of the warm, grilled avocado.

¼ pound small (51 to 60 per pound) raw shrimp, peeled and deveined

½ red bell pepper, chopped

1 teaspoon Old Bay®

Seafood Seasoning

4 ripe, but slightly firm avocados

Chipotle olive oil for brushing

Lime salt to taste

1 medium lime, thinly sliced into 8 slices for garnish

8 cilantro sprigs for garnish

Cooking spray

Preheat the grill to medium, or 350 degrees.

Spray a medium sauté pan with cooking spray and heat to medium heat. Place shrimp, bell pepper, and Old Bay® Seasoning in pan and sauté until shrimp are pink, about 2 to 3 minutes.

Remove from the heat, cover and set aside, keeping warm.

Using a sharp knife, slice avocados in half lengthwise and remove seeds. Using a basting brush, brush insides of avocado generously with olive oil. Sprinkle each halve with about ½ - 1 teaspoon lime salt. Place a grill mat over the grill rack. Place avocado halves on the mat skin side down and grill for 2 minutes. Turn halves over and grill for an additional 4 more minutes.

Using a spoon, fill grilled avocado halves with the shrimp mixture. Garnish with a slice of lime and cilantro sprig. Serve while hot.

TIP: You can find lime salt in specialty spice shops and chipotle olive oil in specialty oil and vinegar shops.

TIP: A grill mat is your grill's next best friend. You can purchase this at a gourmet cooking store or online. A grill mat prevents oil from dripping into your grill, causing flames to ignite and char the avocado. Yes, some oil will spill into the flame, but that is okay.

Squash and Salmon Roll-Ups

MAKES ABOUT 40 ROLL UPS

These roll ups are too big to be eaten all at once, although they are definitely finger food. Pick them up, remove the toothpick and enjoy them in two delicious bites.

8 medium zucchini

1 package (8-ounces) Neufchâtel cheese, room temperature

or

1 package (8-ounces) mascarpone cheese

1 tablespoon capers, rinsed and dried

2 tablespoons deli mustard with horseradish

or

2 tablespoons Dijon-style mustard

Zest of 1 lemon

Juice of 1 lemon, about 3 tablespoons

¼ teaspoon Old Bay® Seafood Seasoning

1 package (8-ounces) cold-smoked salmon, thinly sliced

Dried Dill weed to garnish

Using a knife, cut ends off zucchini. Using a mandolin, slice squash lengthwise, thin enough that squash slices can be rolled without breaking. Continue until all squash are sliced. The 2 outside pieces of each zucchini with outer skin should be reserved for another use.

In a medium bowl, combine cheese, capers, mustard, lemon zest, lemon juice and Old Bay® Seasoning.

On a flat surface like a cutting board, place 1 zucchini slice. Using a knife, spread a thin layer of the cheese mixture the entire length of zucchini. Place 1 slice salmon over the length of the cheese, trimming salmon if necessary. Salmon should cover length of zucchini but not extend over the sides. Roll zucchini up tightly and secure with a toothpick. Sprinkle lightly with dill weed. Prepare roll-ups until remaining ingredients have been used. Cover and chill in the refrigerator until ready to serve.

TIP: This is the perfect appetizer to make for that gluten free, vegetarian guest who will eat seafood. Be sure to buy cold-smoked salmon. It is easier to work with than the drier, more flakey, hot-smoked salmon.

Hot Crabster Brie Dip

MAKES ABOUT 4 CUPS OF HOT DIP

I am not a fan of imitation crab so I don't use it but if you are, feel free to use it. Either way, this is a great recipe for a crowd! Real butter is a must.

1 cup crabmeat, boiled in chicken broth (about 1 ½ pounds King crab legs)

1 cup lobster, boiled in chicken broth (about 2 (8-ounce) lobster tails)

1 round (16-ounces) Brie, cubed, rind intact

1 package (4-ounces) cream cheese, softened

1 tablespoon dry sherry

1 teaspoon Worcestershire® sauce

¼ cup butter, melted

1 baguette, sliced into ¼-inch slices

or

1 focaccia, sliced into ¼-inch slices

Paprika for garnish

Preheat the oven to 350 degrees. In a large bowl, place crab and lobster. In a medium bowl, cream together Brie, cream cheese, sherry, Worcestershire® and butter. Mixture will be chunky. Add the Brie mixture to the crab mixture and mix until blended.

Place the crab mixture in an ovenproof dish, sprinkle lightly with paprika for garnish and bake for 30 minutes, or until warmed through.

Serve in the ovenproof baking dish or in a chafing dish along with baguette/focaccia slices.

Mustard and Herb Encrusted Salmon

SERVES 4

Salmon is a wonderful source of vitamin A, B vitamins and Omega-3 oils as well as being high in protein.

16-ounces wild salmon

¼ cup yellow mustard

Italian seasonings

Lemon slices for garnish

Thyme leaves for garnish

Preheat oven to 350 degrees. Spray ovenproof dish and place salmon inside, skin side down. Spread yellow mustard over the top of salmon. Sprinkle generously with Italian seasoning mixture. Bake 16-20 minutes until salmon is flaky when tested with two forks separating the fish. To serve, carefully remove skin and place on plate. Garnish as desired with lemon slices and thyme leaves.

TIP: Italian seasoning is found in the spice area of grocery stores and is a combination of all the herbs needed for this recipe.

Sautéed Calamari with Roasted Tomato Salsa

MAKES 2 GENEROUS SERVINGS OR 4 SMALL ONES

If you like fried calamari, you will love it sautéed. We ate this in a Vail restaurant after a long day of skiing. We enjoyed it so much I had to duplicate it. I love this salsa recipe as it is quite tasty and doesn't require salt.

FOR THE SALSA:

12 medium tomatoes

2 cloves garlic, unpeeled

1 jalapeño, whole

½ red onion, peeled

Olive oil for drizzling

1½ teaspoons ground cumin

Juice of 2 limes, about 2 tablespoons

¼ cup fresh cilantro, chopped

Preheat the broiler.

Line a jellyroll pan (15 X 10 X 1 inches) with aluminum foil. In the pan, place tomatoes, garlic, jalapeño and red onion. Drizzle lightly with olive oil. Broil vegetables 15 minutes, turning every five minutes. Remove the pan from the oven and let vegetables cool until cool enough to handle.

Remove tomato skins, garlic skins and jalapeño stem and seeds. In a food processor, place tomatoes, garlic, jalapeño, onion, cumin, lime juice and cilantro. Process until blended into a coarse mixture. Set aside.

FOR THE CALAMARI:

16-ounces cleaned squid tubes

¼ cup chipotle olive oil

1 cup reserved salsa

Your favorite bread for dipping

Juice of 1 lemon, about 3 tablespoons

Pat squid dry with paper towels. Using a sharp knife, cut squid tubes into ¼-inch wide ringlets. In a large skillet, place olive oil over a medium heat. Sauté squid ringlets until no longer translucent, about 5 minutes. Add 1 cup salsa and lemon juice to the skillet, stirring until salsa is warm through. Serve in small bowls with favorite bread for dipping into salsa.

TIP: If you have been uncomfortable making calamari because of what you have heard about cleaning squid, don't fret. You can buy squid that has already been cleaned in the Seafood Department at Whole Foods. All you need to do it slice it into ringlets.

Stuffed and Grilled Squid

SERVES 6

Everyone knows about fried calamari, but who eats squid this way? Exactly!
This recipe is sure to be a hit at your next party.

FOR THE CHEESE FILLING:

1 container (8-ounces) burrata cheese

¼ cup Romano cheese, grated

1 jalapeño, seeded and chopped

¼ red bell pepper, seeded and chopped

2 green onions, chopped

½ teaspoon capers, rinsed and dried

1 tablespoon sun-dried tomato, chopped

¼ teaspoon Sriracha® hot sauce

1 clove garlic, minced
½ teaspoon Old Bay®

Seafood Seasoning

Zest of 1 lemon

Juice of 1 lemon, about 3 tablespoons

¼ teaspoon sea salt

Freshly ground pepper, to taste

In a medium bowl, combine burrata, Romano cheese, jalapeño, bell pepper, green onions, capers, sun-dried tomatoes, Sriracha®, garlic, Old Bay® Seasoning, lemon zest, lemon juice and sea salt and season to taste with pepper. Mash the burrata cheese while mixing and blend well.

FOR THE SQUID:

6 intact squid, about 2 ounces each, cleaned with tentacles removed

Cooking spray for prepping

Paprika for garnishing

1 yellow squash, julienned

1 zucchini, julienned

Heat the grill to 425 degrees. Holding a squid in one hand, stuff squid with the cheese filling up to about ½ inch from opening. Secure opening with a toothpick. If overfilled, filling will ooze out while cooking. Repeat with remaining ingredients. Spray squid with cooking spray and sprinkle with paprika. Grill squid for a total of 8 minutes, turning every 2 minutes.

TO SERVE: Remove toothpicks from squid. On a decorative plate, place julienned yellow squash and zucchini. Place squid on julienned veggies.

TIP: After this was photographed, I tried serving this with Hollandaise sauce. That is a keeper! Hollandaise mixes, like Knorr®, which come in an envelope, are easy to prepare as well as tasty; and you don't have to worry about your eggs curdling. Burrata is a very creamy form of fresh mozzarella cheese, found in the deli section of your supermarket or found at Whole Foods.

Spaghetti Squash and Scallops

SERVES 8

The flavors and textures of this little treasure are amazing. Plus, it has an attractive presentation.

TO MARINATE SCALLOPS:

¼ cup lite soy sauce

2 tablespoons honey

1-inch piece fresh ginger, peeled and minced

8 sea scallops, rinsed and drained

In a medium bowl, combine soy sauce, honey, fresh ginger and scallops. Cover and refrigerate.

FOR THE SQUASH:

1 spaghetti squash

Cooking spray for prepping baking sheet

3 cloves garlic, peeled

1 cup Parmesan cheese, finely grated

¼ cup golden raisins

1 tablespoon extra virgin olive oil, butter-flavored if available

1-inch piece fresh ginger, peeled and minced

½ teaspoon ground coriander

¼ teaspoon white pepper

Sea or kosher salt to taste

Preheat the oven to 375 degrees. Using a sharp knife, cut spaghetti squash in half. Using a spoon, scrap out seeds and stringy material in the center. Spray a baking sheet with cooking spray. Place squash cut-sides down on the baking sheet. Wrap garlic cloves in aluminum foil and place on the baking sheet. Bake for 45 minutes. Remove from the oven and cool until squash is cool enough to handle.

Lower the oven temperature to 300 degrees. In a large bowl, combine Parmesan cheese, raisins, olive oil, ginger, coriander and white pepper and season to taste with salt. Using a fork, remove spaghetti strands from the inside of squash and add to the cheese mixture. Remove aluminum foil from garlic cloves. Using a paring knife, cut ends off garlic cloves and place in a small bowl. Using a fork, mash garlic. Add garlic to the squash mixture and stir to combine.

Using 8 (4 ½-inch) cast iron skillets, divide the squash mixture evenly between the skillets. Place the skillets in the oven to keep warm.

TO PREPARE AND SERVE:

Marinated scallops

8 cilantro leaves for garnish

Drain marinade from scallops and discard marinade. Place a medium skillet over medium heat and cook scallops 5 to 7 minutes, or until thoroughly cooked through.

Remove the cast iron skillets from the oven. Place 1 cilantro leaf in the center of each skillet. Top cilantro leaf with 1 scallop. Serve hot.

Roasted Peach Soup with Scallops

MAKES 2 CUPS SOUP

Sweet, salty and crunchy with a presentation that can't be beat. This recipe was a recent favorite at one of my cooking classes. You will understand why when you make it. If you are preparing this for vegetarians, use vegetable broth instead of chicken.

FOR THE SOUP:

Cooking spray for prepping baking sheet

1 can (29-ounces) peaches in water, drained

1/8 cup brown sugar

¾ cup chicken stock or broth

¼ cup milk

1 tablespoon peach-flavored liqueur

1 tablespoon brandy

Reserved peach purée

Pinch ground allspice, less than 1/8 teaspoon

Heaping ¼ teaspoon sea salt

1/8 teaspoon freshly ground black pepper

Preheat the oven to 450 degrees.

On a lightly sprayed, parchment-lined baking sheet, spread drained peaches. Roast for 10 minutes. Remove peaches from the oven and sprinkle with brown sugar. Return peaches to the oven and roast for an additional 10 minutes, stirring occasionally. Remove the baking sheet from the oven and cool peaches slightly on the baking sheet.

In a blender, place peaches with caramelized brown sugar and any drippings and process until smooth. Set aside.

In a medium kettle, simmer chicken stock, milk, liqueur and brandy over a low heat. Add peach purée and season to taste with allspice, salt and pepper. Remove the kettle from the heat, cover and keep warm.

Roasted Peach Soup
with Scallops continued

TO SERVE:

1 bay scallop per person served, rinsed and drained

Sea salt to taste

Freshly ground black pepper to taste

1 to 2 tablespoons extra virgin olive oil

Aged-balsamic vinegar for garnish

Peanuts, toasted and coarsely chopped for garnish

Pat scallops dry with paper towels. Season them to taste with salt and pepper. Place olive oil in a sauté pan over medium-high heat. When a few drops of water sprinkled into the pan splatter, the oil is ready. Place scallops in the pan and sauté 2 minutes without moving. Turn scallops over and sauté an additional 2 minutes, or until scallops are golden brown and their sides look opaque.

To serve, place soup in individual Chinese ceramic soup spoons, one spoon per guest.

Top soup with 1 scallop, drizzle with balsamic vinegar and sprinkle with peanuts. (See photo.)

TRIVIA: Bay scallops are small and sea scallops are large. If only sea scallops are available, cut them into fourths for this recipe.

TIP: Any remaining soup is great over vegetables or even mixed into pasta.

TIP: To toast peanuts, place peanuts in a small skillet over a medium heat. Stir often to keep them from burning, about 5 minutes. No oil needed.

Cheese

Apricot, Brie and Craisin Crostini

MAKES ABOUT 10 CROSTINI

1 large yam – choose one that is as cylindrical as possible

5 dried apricots, chopped into small pieces

Extra virgin olive oil

30 craisins

4-ounces Brie, sliced into thin pieces

½ cup apricot jam

Dried thyme for garnish

Peel yam, brush with extra virgin olive oil, place in glass baking dish and cook in microwave ten minutes at power 8 (out of 10.) Don't overcook or it will be too soft to serve as base for the crostinis. Cool, slice into ¼-inch circles.

Preheat oven to 350 degrees. Place yam slices in an unsprayed ovenproof dish. Layer on a piece of Brie (cut to fit,) dollop of jam, apricots and 3 craisins. Sprinkle with thyme. Repeat with all remaining ingredients.

Bake 5 minutes until cheese is soft. Serve warm.

TIP: This gluten free crostini with healthy yam base is a keeper.

TRIVIA: Craisins are dried cranberries and are easily found near raisins.

Zucchini and Cheese Curd Bites

MAKES ABOUT 20 LITTLE BITES

Cheese curds are a Wisconsin favorite. If you aren't able to locate curds or order them online, just use 1-inch squares of Cheddar cheese and sprinkle the cheese with dill. There are only two ingredients in this one—it doesn't get much easier.

2 medium zucchini

1 package (4-ounces) garlic
and dill cheese curds

Preheat the oven to 350 degrees. Using a sharp knife, slice zucchini into ½-inch circles and cut out seedy core. Reserve the centers for another use.

On an ungreased baking sheet, place the slices of zucchini. Place a curd in the center of each zucchini, filling the hole so cheese is level with zucchini. Bake for 8 minutes. Cool for 2 minutes and then serve. Cooling slightly will prevent the cheese from oozing out the bottom.

TIP: When filling zucchini rings with curds, try to imagine how the cheese will melt over the top. This will help with its placement.

TRIVIA: Do you know how to check the authenticity of a cheese curd? It has to squeak in your teeth as you bite into it.

"Fondue" for Two

SERVES 2

The ingredients in this recipe are what you find in a traditional Swiss fondue. This is a much easier preparation, yet it has the same wonderful flavors. Gruyere is a hard, nutty cheese. If it is not available, just use one fitting that description. Some possibilities are Swiss, fontina, Gouda, or Emmentaler.

2 medium zucchini

1 large garlic clove, minced

6 ounces Gruyere cheese, cut into cubes

1 tablespoon white wine

1 teaspoon Kirschwasser®, cherry brandy, literally "cherry water" in German

Ground nutmeg to taste

Freshly ground black pepper to taste

1 baguette, sliced into ¼-inch slices

1 apple, cored and sliced

dill cheese curds

Preheat the broiler. In 2 (5-inch) cast iron skillets, sprinkle equal amounts of minced garlic. Add equal amounts of cheese to each skillet. Pour ½ tablespoon wine and of ½ teaspoon Kirschwasser® into each cheese-filled skillet. Season to taste with nutmeg and pepper.

Place the skillets about 5 inches from the broiler and broil 8 minutes, or until lightly browned on top. Cool for 5 minutes. Serve hot with baguette and apple slices for dippers.

TIP: Cheese will thicken up as it cools, which does not affect the flavor.

Grilled Watermelon and Goat Cheese Bites

MAKES 20 TO 30 BITES

We were treated to these eclectic bites at a catered, museum cocktail party. Naturally, I had to take a photo and attempt to replicate them.

FOR THE TOMATO CONCASSÉ:

2 large tomatoes

2 teaspoons extra virgin olive oil

1 teaspoon red wine vinegar

1/3 cup fresh basil leaves, chopped

Fill a large bowl with ice water and set aside. Using a sharp knife, core and make an X on the bottom of tomatoes. Drop tomato into boiling water for 10 seconds and remove. Peel tomatoes and immerse in icy cold water to retard cooking. Using a sharp knife, seed and chop tomatoes.

In a medium bowl, combine tomatoes, olive oil, vinegar, and basil. Cover with plastic wrap and refrigerate until ready to use.

½ cup almonds, chopped

1 tablespoon sugar

In a small, heavy ungreased skillet, place almonds and sugar over medium heat. Stir to combine.

Continue to stir frequently until nuts are golden brown. Set aside until ready to assemble bites.

FOR THE WATERMELON:

1 medium watermelon

Preheat the grill to high. Using a sharp knife, slice watermelon into 1-inch slices. Using a 2-inch biscuit cutter, cut biscuit-like watermelon circles from each slice. Repeat until you have desired number of pieces. Grill watermelon pieces about

1 ½ minutes per side, 3 minutes total. Remove pieces from the grill and cool. Using a melon baller, make a small well in the top of each watermelon piece. Reserve balls for a snack later.

Grilled Watermelon continued

TO ASSEMBLE THE BITES:

8 ounces goat cheese

Reserved almonds

¼ cup tawny port

Fresh basil leaves for garnish

Assemble by filling each watermelon well with ½ teaspoon of goat cheese, 1 teaspoon tomato concassé, and sprinkle almonds over the top.

Pour port into a measuring cup. Insert a straw into the cup and fill the straw about ½ inch with port. Place finger over the top of the straw to hold liquid. Place the straw over watermelon well and release port, drizzling it over the top of the cheese mixture. Garnish with a basil leaf and place in metallic-lined paper muffin liner to serve.

TIP: Concassé is French for "rough chop". This preparation is often used for tomatoes. When prepared this way, tomatoes are peeled, seeded and chopped. Concassé is the term often used when making bruschetta.

Baked Brie with Toasted Almonds and Preserves

SERVES 6 TO 10

Sweet, crunchy and creamy—this covers a lot of bases.

1 wheel Brie (13-ounces), skin intact

½ cup slivered almonds, toasted (salted or unsalted)

½ cup preserves – Use your favorite!

Preheat the oven to 375 degrees.

Place Brie in a baking dish, cover Brie with preserves, sprinkle almonds over top. Bake for 15 minutes, or until soft. Serve with your favorite crackers.

TIP: In the fall I use apricot jam and at Christmas I use raspberry. Coordinating the color of the preserves with the occasion or time of year adds flair to what you serve.

TIP: Place slivered almonds into a preheated medium frying pan and heat until slightly browned. Still often taking care not to let them burn. No oil is necessary as nuts have enough of their own.

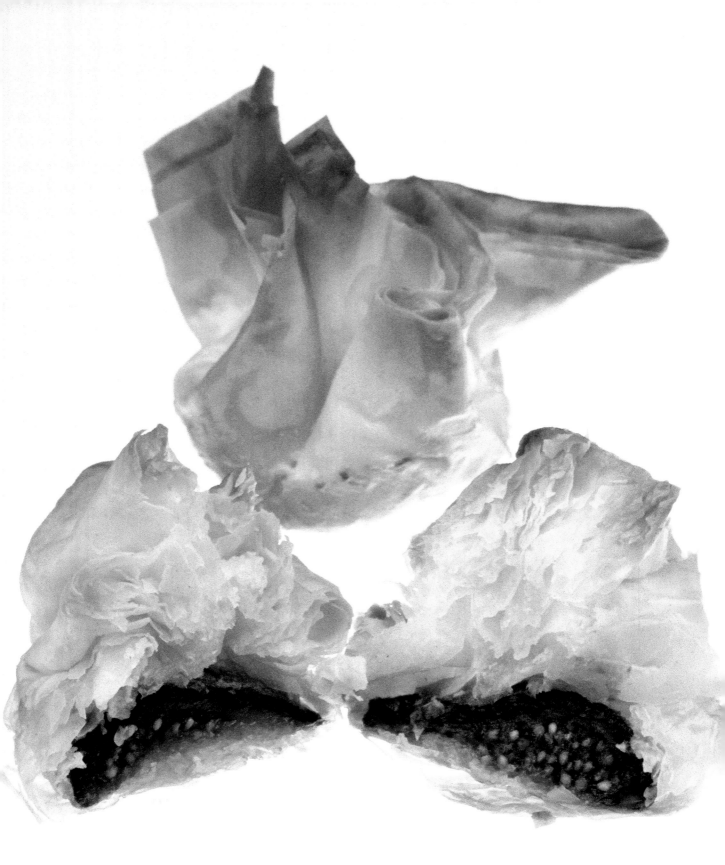

Fig Mascarpone Bundles

MAKES 30 APPETIZERS

My husband and I attended a wine tasting at an upscale restaurant where an array of appetizers was served. When I bit into their version of a fig mascarpone bundle, time stood still. What a tasty treat this was with a surprise in the middle. It impressed me so much I had to sample two more to figure out how to duplicate it at home. The result is a keeper.

20 sheets or ½ package phyllo dough, or pre-made phyllo cups

¾ cup butter, melted

15 dried figs, cut in half

1 package (8-ounces) mascarpone cheese

Preheat the oven to 350 degrees. Spread one sheet of phyllo dough out onto a cutting board. Using a pastry brush, lightly dab sheet with melted butter. Layer a second sheet on top and again lightly dab with butter. Repeat, layering third sheet on top and again lightly dabbing with butter. Layer fourth sheet on top but do not dab with butter. Using a pizza cutter, cut the rectangular-shaped dough into 6 squares. Gently separate each square.

In the center of each square, place ½ dried fig and 1 teaspoon mascarpone cheese. Using the same pastry brush, "paint" melted butter around the four edges of the square then gather the four corners up over the fig, pinching the edges and corners together. Repeat with remaining dough until all halved figs have been used.

Place bundles in unlined and ungreased mini muffin tins. Dab a little butter on top of each bundle, which helps them turn a beautiful caramel brown. Bake for 12 minutes until lightly browned. Cool for 5 minutes and then serve hot.

TIP: If time is an issue, use the premade phyllo cups, which are also delicious. Just do not heat them in the microwave as they will become mushy. Pre-made phyllo cups are often a seasonal item in some grocery stores.

TIP: If figs are unavailable, try dried apricots. Both are so good you can't go wrong.

Beet and Goat Cheese Skewers

MAKES 12 TO 15 SKEWERS

Beets and lemon are wonderful partners!

3 fresh beets

Extra virgin olive oil cooking spray

Salt to taste

Freshly ground black pepper to taste

1 log (4-ounces) goat cheese

2 tablespoons fresh lemon zest

Aged balsamic vinegar

Preheat the oven to 350 degrees. Cut off beet greens and either discard or wash them, place in a plastic bag, and refrigerate for another use. Scrub beets with a vegetable brush. Using a vegetable peeler, peel beets. Using a sharp knife, cut beets into quarters. Place beets in an oven-proof glass dish, spray with extra virgin olive oil cooking spray, sprinkle with salt and roast 45 to 60 minutes, or until beets can be easily pierced with a sharp knife. Remove from the oven and cool completely. When beets are cooled, using a sharp knife, cut beets into ½ to ¾ inch pieces.

Cut goat cheese into pieces and roll in to ½ to ¾ inch balls. Place lemon zest on a plate and roll each goat cheese ball in zest.

Thread mini skewers (4 to 6 inches long) with beet, cheese ball, beet. Repeat with the remaining ingredients. Drizzle a serving plate large enough to accommodate skewers with aged balsamic vinegar. Place skewers on top of balsamic vinegar.

This recipe may be made 8 hours ahead, saving you one less thing to do at the last minute. Cover with plastic wrap and refrigerate until ready to serve. This recipe is best served at room temperature to bring out the flavor of the cheese. Remove from the refrigerator about 1 hour prior to serving.

Caprese Tower

SERVES 2

Can you ever get too much "Caprese" anything? This is such a fantastic combination of flavors that any shape or presentation of it is a winner!

2 medium tomatoes, cored

4 slices fresh mozzarella cheese, ¼ inch in thickness

4 tablespoons prepared basil pesto

Aged balsamic vinegar for drizzling

6 basil leaves for garnish

Sea salt or Kosher salt to taste

Using a mandoline, slice tomatoes between 1/8-inch and ¼-inch thick. Choose 10 of the best slices, reserving the others for another use.

On a plate, begin the tower by layering tomato slice, cheese slice, tomato slice, 1 tablespoon pesto, tomato slice, cheese slice, tomato slice, 1 tablespoon pesto and top is a tomato slice.

Repeat the same steps making the second tower.

Drizzle balsamic vinegar over the top, garnish with basil leaves and season to taste with salt.

TIP: A mandoline is a hand-operated machine with various adjustable blades. It can be used for slicing or for julienne or French-fry cutting. It is very sharp and cuts with uniformity and precision. This gadget is worth having.

TIP: To be considered traditional aged balsamic, balsamic vinegar must be aged at least 12 years. Most balsamic vinegar you purchase at the supermarket is a commercial variety and isn't aged. You can use a commercial brand, but it won't be as sweet or syrupy as an aged product.

Cheese Crackers with Blackberry Preserves

MAKES ABOUT 15 CRACKERS

Sweet, salty and gluten free! Make as much or as little as needed!

The crackers can be made in advance, but if you do so, put the preserves on at the last minute so the crackers stay crispy.

4-ounces Pecorino Romano cheese, grated (or any hard cheese will work)

4-ounces Blackberry Lavender Preserves or your favorite fruit spread, jam or preserves

Preheat the oven to 400 degrees. Place 1 tablespoon grated cheese on an ungreased baking sheet about 2 inches apart. They will spread as they bake. Bake 5 to 7 minutes, or until they begin to brown slightly around the edges. Cool 5 minutes on baking sheet to finish crisping, then transfer to a wire cooling rack.

Place 1 teaspoon of blackberry lavender preserves on each cracker. Place crackers on a platter to serve.

TIP: Make these 2 days ahead of time and store in air-tight container in the refrigerator. Place preserves on top at last minute.

TIP: The blackberry lavender preserves can be found at specialty gourmet cooking shops and at farmers' markets. If a substitution is needed, no worries. Raspberry jam is really good too!

Fig and Lemon Bruschetta

MAKES ABOUT 20 BRUSCHETTA

Fresh lemon combined with mascarpone cheese is a delicious combination.
Topping it with the sweetness of fig is perfect!

1 (12-ounces) plain or sourdough baguette

Extra virgin olive oil for brushing

1 large lemon, washed

Juice from lemon (about 3 tablespoons)

1 tub (8-ounces) mascarpone cheese

1 jar (8-ounces) fig spread

Preheat the oven to 350 degrees. Using a serrated knife, slice baguette into ¼ to ½-inch slices. Place slices on a baking sheet and brush (or spray) one side lightly with olive oil. Bake for 4 minutes, or until lightly golden. Cool on baking sheet.

Using a citrus zester, zest long strands from lemon and set aside.

In a medium bowl, combine mascarpone and lemon juice. Using a knife, spread the cheese mixture on toasted side of baguette slices. Spread about a tablespoon fig spread on top of the cheese mixture. Garnish with lemon zest.

Serve at room temperature.

TIP: This can be served as a dessert as well as an appetizer. For a dessert, substitute a graham cracker square for the toasted baguette. It's like having a personal cheesecake.

Lemon Lavender Burrata

MAKES ONE 8-OUNCE BURRATA

I enjoy lemon and lavender together. Blending them with this creamy cheese makes a wonderful, summer small plate. I used this recipe for my Los Angeles audition for the national show, "Master Chef's Next Best Home Cook." The judge liked my presentation and flavors, but the interview went south when she asked me how I make burrata. She marked me down because I don't make it from scratch. I do make most things from scratch, but burrata is just so delicious, why try to re-create perfection?

1 container (8-ounces) burrata cheese

Reserved burrata casing

½ cup mascarpone cheese

1 ½ teaspoons honey

3 tablespoons fresh lemon zest

3 teaspoons fresh lemon juice

1 baguette

½ teaspoon dried lavender, crushed with mortar and pestle

Aged Balsamic Vinegar for drizzling

Drain water from burrata cheese and place cheese on a cutting board. Using a paring knife, gently slice a 4-inch slit on the underside of burrata. Using a small spoon, carefully scoop out cheese, leaving casing intact. Reserve casing.

In a medium bowl with high sides, place inner cheese. Add mascarpone, honey, lemon zest, lemon juice, and lavender. Using an electric mixer, whip the burrata mixture until light and fluffy.

Using a spoon, gently scoop the burrata mixture back into the burrata casing, overfilling it a bit. You will have excess burrata mixture, so reserve any surplus for the next day to enjoy with crackers.

On a serving plate, place the filled burrata slit side down. Cover and chill in the refrigerator until ready to serve.

Preheat the oven to 350 degrees. Using a bread knife, slice baguette diagonally into ½-inch slices. On a baking sheet, place slices and bake for 5 minutes, or until slices are lightly golden.

TO SERVE: This recipe can be served cold or at room temperature. Drizzle burrata with balsamic vinegar just before serving with toasted baguette slices and a side salad or shredded vegetables for color.

TIP: Burrata is found in supermarkets and specialty food stores next to the fresh mozzarella. In Italian, burrata translates to "butter". If you haven't tried it before, you really should. Made from both mozzarella and cream and resembling a mozzarella ball, burrata is filled with a soft, stringy curd and cheese. It has a milky, buttery flavor. Lavender can be purchased at specialty spice stores if it is not available at your favorite grocery store.

Caprese Pinwheels

MAKES 10 TO 12 SPIRALS

My guests loved this recipe the first time I served it! The possibilities are endless with a mozzarella roll. Also, if you haven't purchased a basil plant, I recommend doing so! I use mine in so many recipes that I need it growing and available in my kitchen at all times! Basil plants are more available in the spring and summer months. Do not over water basil.

1 package (12-ounces) fresh mozzarella roll/sheet

1/3 cup prepared basil pesto

1 large tomato

Aged balsamic vinegar

10 to 12 basil leaves for garnish

Carefully unwrap the cheese roll onto a cutting board. Using a knife, spread pesto evenly over cheese. Using a mandolin, thinly slice tomato. Place tomato slices evenly over pesto.

Starting at the narrow end, tightly roll cheese until the opposite end is reached. Wrap the rolled cheese tightly in plastic wrap and chill in the refrigerator until ready to serve.

When ready to serve, using a sharp knife, slice the rolled cheese log into 10 to 12 spirals. Using 10 to 12 small appetizer plates, drizzle balsamic vinegar over each plate. Place 1 spiral on each plate and garnish with a basil leaf.

TIP: If you haven't purchased a mozzarella roll, it can be described as a flat sheet of mozzarella. It is found in the deli section of your supermarket near the fresh mozzarella balls.

Cheesy Beer Dip with Ranch Pretzels

MAKES 3 POUNDS OF PRETZELS AND 2 CUPS OF DIP

My Ranch Pretzels are yummy by themselves, so don't feel guilty if you don't make the dip. The dip recipe is enough to accommodate about half the pretzels. If you want enough dip for all the pretzels, double the recipe.

FOR THE CHEESY BEER DIP:

2 packages (8-ounces) cream cheese, softened (You can use light Neufchatel.)

1 package (1-ounce) Hidden Valley® Ranch Dressing Mix

¾ can (9-ounces) your favorite beer

2 cups shredded Cheddar cheese, lightly packed

In a large bowl, combine cream cheese, ranch dressing mix, beer, and Cheddar cheese. Cover with plastic wrap and refrigerate for several hours or overnight. The cream cheese mixture may be a little soupy but thickens as it chills.

FOR THE RANCH PRETZELS:

3 packages (16-ounces) pretzel twists

1 bottle (10-ounces) Orville Redenbacher® Popping & Topping Oil

1 package (1-ounce) Hidden Valley® Ranch Dressing Mix

1 to 2 tablespoons lemon pepper, or to taste

Place pretzels in a large plastic bag. A white kitchen garbage bag works well. This is best done outside as the oil may leak through the bag while mixing. Drizzle oil over pretzels and mix to coat, turning and shaking the bag several times. Add dressing mix and lemon pepper and continue turning and shaking the bag until pretzels are evenly coated. Store seasoned pretzels in a large, air-tight bowl or several plastic zip-loc bags. Let pretzels sit for a couple of hours before eating. Pretzels will keep for several weeks.

Brie in Puff Pastry

SERVES 8 TO 10

Use any flavor of jam in this recipe you have on hand. I like raspberry at Christmastime and apricot in the Fall. Once again, there are no rules, so just have fun.

1 sheet frozen puff pastry sheet, or half of 1 package (17.3-ounces)

Flour for flouring surface

1 round (8-ounces) Brie, rind intact

½ cup apricot preserves or raspberry jam

2 dashes Chipotle Tabasco®, optional

1/3 cup dried cranberries or currants

¼ cup sliced almonds, toasted

Milk for brushing pastry

Crackers (multigrain are nice)

Sliced apples

Preheat the oven to 400 degrees. Thaw pastry sheet at room temperature for about 30 minutes. Unfold pastry on to a lightly floured surface. Using a rolling pin, roll pastry sheet into 1 square, approximately 14 inches in diameter.

Place Brie in the center of puff pastry.

In a small bowl, combine preserves or jam and chipotle sauce. Using a knife, spread the jam mixture over the Brie. Layer cranberries or currants on top of jam, and almonds on top of cranberries or currants.

Bring two opposite corners of the pastry up over the Brie until they just meet, then bring the other two corners to the center so that all 4 corners touch, covering the Brie. Gently pinch the edges together to seal shut. Brush the entire pastry with milk, which will help it brown nicely.

Bake for 20 minutes, or until golden. Let stand 1 hour before serving with crackers and sliced, crispy apples.

Apple, Brie and Rosemary Tarts

MAKES 6 TARTS

I pair three of my favorite flavors into this light and fresh treat.

1 package (11-ounces) frozen French bread dough, thawed

1 round (8-ounces) Brie, rind left on, chopped into ½ inch cubes

1 large apple, peel left on, cored and chopped into ½ inch cubes

1 tablespoon fresh rosemary, chopped

Freshly ground black pepper to taste

Cooking spray

Place the oven rack in the middle of the oven. Preheat the oven to 350 degrees. Spray six (3.5-inch) cast iron skillets with cooking spray. Divide the dough into six balls. Flatten the dough balls, then press each ball into the bottoms and up the sides of each cast iron skillet. Mold the dough so that it comes just to the top edge of each skillet.

In a medium bowl, combine Brie and apple and toss to combine. Place 1/6 of the apple-Brie mixture in the center of each cast iron skillet. Sprinkle each pan with 1/6 rosemary and season to taste with pepper.

Bake for 15 minutes, or until pastry is golden and Brie is melted.

FOR THE GARNISH: Fresh rosemary

Buy enough fresh rosemary to separate out six pretty tips to use as garnish.

TIP: These cast iron skillets can be found in gourmet cooking stores or online.

Blackened Brie with Toasted Walnuts

SERVES 8 TO 12

If you are a fan of blackened fish, you will love this one!

1 tablespoon hot, Smokey Spanish paprika

2 teaspoons dry mustard

1 teaspoon cayenne

1 teaspoon ground cumin

1 teaspoon roasted garlic powder

1 teaspoon dried thyme leaves

1 teaspoon freshly ground black pepper

1 teaspoon white pepper

1 round (16-ounces) Brie, rind intact

½ cup walnuts, coarsely chopped and toasted

Milk for brushing Brie

In a small bowl, combine paprika, mustard, cayenne, cumin, roasted garlic powder, thyme, black pepper and white pepper. Place the spice mixture on a plate that is flat and larger than the Brie. Using a pastry brush, brush all sides of the Brie with milk. Place Brie on the plate with the seasonings and press into seasonings. Roll the sides and and flip over to coat the bottom of Brie in the spices. Press the seasoning into Brie as much as possible. The milk will allow the dry seasonings to adhere to the Brie.

Preheat the oven to 375 degrees. Place Brie in ovenproof, decorative dish slightly larger than the Brie and bake for 20 minutes, or until Brie is soft when cut into. Sprinkle the walnuts over the top and serve hot with crackers and tart apple slices.

Green Olive Tapenade Bruschetta

MAKES 1 CUP OR ENOUGH FOR 15 TO 20 BRUSCHETTA

This is seriously the easiest recipe I have created in a long time

1 jar (4-ounces) green, pitted olives (no pimentos)

3 tablespoons pine nuts, toasted

3 ounces blue cheese, crumbled

3 tablespoons extra virgin olive oil

1 clove garlic

1 (12-ounces) plain or sourdough baguette, ready to bake

In a food processor, place olives, pine nuts, blue cheese, olive oil and garlic. Process until chunky. Transfer to a bowl, cover with plastic wrap and refrigerate until ready to serve.

Preheat oven to temperature indicated on baguette package. Bake 8 minutes and cool on wire rack. Using a serrated knife, slice ½ inch slices of bread on the diagonal.

Using a butter knife, spread the green olive tapenade on baguette slices and serve.

TIP: This tapenade can be made a few days ahead of time. The day of the gathering, spread it over the bruschetta, plate, cover with plastic wrap and chill until ready to serve. This is one less task to do at the last minute.

Himalayan Salt Block Cooking

Useful Himalayan Salt Block Tips

- Bring salt blocks up to heat slowly so as to release the water from them and prevent them from cracking. Place in cold oven or on cold grill and set heat for 200 degrees. Once reached, keep at this temperature about 15 minutes. Then raise to 300 degrees and leave for 15 more minutes. Continue at this pace until the desired temperature is reached. "Low and slow." (If grilling, block may also be heated in oven and then brought out to hot grill.)

- Cool block overnight before cleaning. Only use water and brush to clean food debris off. Salt is antimicrobial so does not need soap.

- Store salt block in dry environment.

- Do not add salt to any recipe using salt block or your food will be way too salty!

- Keep in mind that the more moisture in your food used, the more salt it will pick up.

- Oil does not count for above "moisture" comment as oil repels salt and keeps it from being absorbed as much as a watery liquid will.

- Chill a block in freezer for a couple of hours if planning to use it for ice cream or for a serving plate.

- Heated salt blocks will darken so if you want to use one for a pretty serving platter, you need to own more than one like I do!

- Metal holders for your salt blocks are available and recommended, making handling a hot block so much easier and safer. Plus, over time a piece may break off on a cleavage line and the holder keeps it intact enough to keep using it.

Coconut-Curry Shrimp

6 TO 8 SMALL PLATE SERVINGS

I bought The Salt Plate Cookbook by Williams-Sonoma and love this method of cooking. This is a recipe adapted from it. A salt block is a must in every kitchen!

½ cup coconut milk (I prefer lite.)

4 teaspoons curry powder

½ teaspoon garlic powder

½ teaspoon onion powder

½ teaspoon ground ginger

½ teaspoon ground cumin

½ teaspoon dried savory

¼ teaspoon cayenne pepper

Zest of 1 medium lime

1 tablespoon fresh lime juice (or one lime)

1 pound wild shrimp, peeled and deveined, tails removed

Place a salt plate on a gas grill or in the oven on low, 250 degrees, about 15 minutes. Increase the temperature of the grill or oven to medium, 350 degrees, for another 15 minutes. Then, once again, increase the temperature of the grill or oven to 500 degrees and wait another 15 minutes before cooking.

While the plate is heating, make the marinade. In a medium bowl, combine coconut milk, curry powder, garlic powder, onion powder, ginger, cumin, savory, cayenne pepper, lime zest and lime juice. Add shrimp, toss to coat and marinate for 8 to 10 minutes.

Remove the salt plate from the oven and place on a trivet on the counter. Using tongs to grab the shrimp, place shrimp on the hot salt plate and cook 1 to 2 minutes per side, or until shrimp are pink and firm. Discard the marinade. Serve immediately.

TIP: The shrimp will sizzle and be a show-stopper. The block will stay hot for several hours so do not be in a hurry to clean it.

Pistachio and Garlic Baked Brie

SERVES 4 TO 6

Cooking with a Himalayan salt block is the latest trend. It can be used not only for grilling and chilling food but also serving as well. My Pistachio and Garlic Baked Brie cooked using this latest technique offers crunch, spice, creamy, soft cheese, a hint of salt and the sweetness of fruit.

1/4 cup pistachios, unsalted and shelled

2 tablespoons almonds, unsalted

1 large clove garlic

½ teaspoon smoky paprika

Freshly ground black pepper to taste

1 tablespoon milk

1 wheel (8-ounces) Brie, rind intact

12 dates, pitted

12 grape skewers, red seedless, 3 grapes per 4-inch skewer

1 Granny Smith or Fuji apple, cored and sliced

1 baguette, sliced into 2-inch thick slices

Place a salt block (6 by 8 inches or 8 by 8 inches) in a cold oven and turn the temperature to 200 degrees. Heat the salt block for 15 minutes, then increase the oven temperature to 300 degrees. Heat the salt block for an additional 15 minutes, then increase the oven temperature to 350 degrees. This slow heating of the block allows water to escape and prevents the salt block from cracking. Low and slow is the way to go.

While the block is heating, in a food processor, place pistachios, almonds, garlic, paprika and pepper and process until crumbly. Cut a piece of waxed paper larger than Brie. Spread the pistachio mixture over the waxed paper circle. Using a pastry brush, brush all side of Brie with milk. Roll Brie in the pistachio mixture until all of the nut mixture is used.

Place a trivet on the counter and remove the salt block from the oven. Place the block on the trivet. Place Brie in the center of the block. Place dates and grape skewers on the salt block surrounding the cheese. Return the salt block to the oven for 10 minutes, or until cheese is soft. Place the salt block on a trivet for serving. Serve apple slices and bread slices on the side.

TIP: *You can find unsalted and shelled pistachios in bulk at most health food stores.*

TIP: *The grapes and dates cooked on the block grab a little salty flavor to keep it interesting.*

Julienne-Style Vegetables

SERVES 4

Julienne vegetables is an easy way to achieve uniform-sized pieces. The preparation used in this recipe allows veggies to retain a bright color and a little crunch with just a hint of salt.

1/2 pound zucchini

1/2 pound carrots

¼ cup or so favorite olive oil (I like Roasted Almond Extra Virgin Olive Oil.)

Freshly ground black pepper to taste

Place a salt block inside a cold oven and then set the oven temperature to 200 degrees. Heat the oven and the salt block up slowly, over 30 minutes, raising the temperature 100 degrees every ten minutes until it reaches 400 degrees.

Using a shredder designed to julienne vegetables, julienne carrots and zucchini into 2 to 3-inch long pieces. In a medium bowl, place shredded carrots and zucchini. Drizzle with just enough olive oil to coat lightly. Toss gently.

Remove the salt block from the oven and place the hot block on trivets on the countertop. Using tongs, place vegetables on the salt block and cook briefly, mixing constantly, no more than 1 minute. Season to taste with freshly ground black pepper.

Remove from the salt block and serve. Do not allow veggies to linger on the salt block too long or they will pick up too much salt.

TIP: Julienne strips are thin, 1/8-inch thick, matchstick strips. They can be any length you choose. A julienne tool may be found at gourmet cooking shops. It is very similar to a potato peeler with extra notches on the cutting part.

Chocolate Fondue in a Himalayan Salt Bowl

SERVES 4 TO 6

A salt bowl presentation is tough to beat. Because it holds the heat, there is no need for a traditional fondue pot with a flame underneath. If there is any leftover chocolate, be sure to remove it from the bowl and store it in another container as salt will continue to wick into the fondue.

6-ounces dark Mercken® chocolate

1/3 cup half and half

½ teaspoon coconut liqueur

1 tablespoon coconut oil

Assortment of dippers: cubed

angel food cake, strawberries, sliced apples, marshmallows, be creative

Place the salt bowl in a cold oven and set the temperature to 250 degrees. After 10 minutes, increase the temperature to 350 degrees. Keep the salt bowl at this temperature while working on the chocolate and until ready to use.

Break chocolate in to equally sized pieces. Place the chocolate and the half and half in the top of a double boiler. Fill the bottom of a double boiler with an inch or two of water and set the pan over medium heat. Water in the bottom of the double boiler should never touch the top and reach a gentle boil. Stir the chocolate mixture frequently until melted. When the chocolate mixture is smooth, remove the top of the double boiler from the heat and add liqueur and oil. Stir to combine. Pour the chocolate mixture into the salt bowl and serve immediately with dippers and fancy toothpicks. Place the hot bowl on a trivet to protect the table.

TIP: Change it up and have fun with this one. Try Kahlua®, Bailey's® Irish Crème, Amaretto®. This list is endless. There you go. Now you have more than one recipe.

TIP: Do not melt chocolate in the salt bowl or the result will be a really salty fondue. Trust me! The above method yields a nice hint of salt, but it will not be overwhelming.

TIP: Mercken® chocolate may be found online or at specialty baking shops. But don't let that scare you off – regular semisweet chocolate chips will do the job as well!

Salt Block Ice Cream Sundae

SERVES 2

I can guarantee your guests have never eaten this type of sundae. They will love the process of preparing it as much as the flavors. Since I own several salt blocks—when I find something good, look out—I keep one in the freezer ready for that emergency dessert.

1 semisweet chocolate bar

Vanilla bean ice cream, slightly softened

¼ cup unsalted nuts (any kind), chopped

Reserved 3 tablespoons chocolate shavings

¼ cup chocolate sauce

or

¼ cup caramel sauce

Chill a salt block for at least 2 hours in the freezer.

Using a vegetable peeler or grater, shave 3 tablespoons of chocolate shavings from chocolate bar. Set aside.

Place a kitchen towel on the counter. Remove the salt block from the freezer and place it on the kitchen towel.

Using an ice cream scoop, spoon 2 scoops of ice cream onto the chilled salt block. Using a rubber scraper, stir ice cream and smash it down on the salt block. Using the rubber scraper, blend in nuts, chocolate shavings and sauce into the ice cream. Work quickly so ice creams picks up some salt but not too much. The longer the ice cream sits on the salt block, the more salt flavor it will acquire. Scoop ice cream into individual dishes to serve.

TIP: This is also delicious made with a combination of both chocolate and caramel sauces. If you chose to use both, substitute 1/8 cup of each.

Desserts

Classic Oatmeal Chocolate Chip Cookies

Skillet Cranberry Scones

Craisin, Pistachio and White Chocolate Biscotti

Russian Tea Cakes

Chocolate Dipped Strawberries

Sweet Espresso Almonds

Mini Molten Chocolate Cakes

Cookies and Cream Truffles

Caramel Apple Fruit Dip

Brownie and Strawberry Kabobs Drizzled with Chocolate

Vanilla Sugar

Rice Pudding with Caramelized Vanilla Sugar Topping

Festive Fruit Pizza

Bread Pudding with Rum Sauce

Oatmeal Chocolate Chip Banana Bread

Spicy Crème Brulee

Monster Cookies

Classic Oatmeal Chocolate Chip Cookies

MAKES ABOUT 50 COOKIES

¾ cup butter, softened

1 cup brown sugar

½ cup granulated sugar

1 egg, beaten

¼ cup water

1 ½ teaspoon vanilla extract

1 cup unbleached flour

½ teaspoon baking soda

1 teaspoon ground cinnamon

1 teaspoon salt

1 cup semisweet chocolate chips

3 cups old fashioned oats

Preheat the oven to 335* degrees. In a large bowl and using an electric mixer, cream together butter and sugars. Add egg, water and vanilla and mix well. In another large bowl, combine flour, baking soda, cinnamon and salt. Add dry ingredients to the sugar mixture and beat thoroughly, until a smooth cookie dough is formed. Stir in chocolate chips and oats.

*No typo—that's really 335 degrees!

Cover the bowl with plastic wrap and chill in the refrigerator for 30 minutes. Line a cookie sheet with parchment paper. Scoop dough by rounded tablespoons onto cookie sheet and bake for 11 minutes, or until lightly golden. Cool 5 minutes on pan, then transfer to wire rack.

TIP: Use a tablespoon-sized ice cream scoop for easy measuring and consistency.

Skillet Cranberry Scones

MAKES 6 LARGE SCONES

This sweet, tart treat has an attractive presentation and is tasty as well. Enjoy it for dessert, breakfast, a snack or just because. Who says you have to go out for brunch to make it special?

3 ¼ cups all-purpose flour

¼ cup granulated sugar

4 teaspoons baking powder

½ teaspoon baking soda

½ teaspoon salt

½ cup butter

¾ cup fresh cranberries, chopped, juices retained

1/3 cup granulated sugar

Zest of 1 orange

2/3 cup buttermilk

1 large egg, beaten

1/3 cup walnuts, chopped

Preheat the oven to 375 degrees. In a large bowl, combine flour, ¼ cup sugar, baking powder, baking soda and salt. Using 2 knives or a pastry blender, cut in butter until the flour mixture becomes crumbly. In another medium bowl, combine cranberries, 1/3 cup sugar and orange zest. Add buttermilk, egg and nuts to the cranberry mixture and stir to blend. Add the cranberry mixture to the flour mixture and stir until just blended.

In 6 ungreased (4-inch) cast iron skillets, divide the dough evenly and mound in the center of each pan. Bake for 25 minutes, or until the tops of the scones are golden brown. Serve warm with butter, if desired.

TIP: Fresh cranberries are available in late fall and during the winter. Stock up and freeze them for year-round use. No special preparation needed. Just freeze them in the bags they come in.

Craisin, Pistachio & White Chocolate Biscotti

MAKES ABOUT 2 DOZEN

Need a gift for that hard-to-buy for person? Here you go! Just wrap these up in a clear bag with some pretty ribbon, and you are set! Include a coffee mug for a really special touch.

3 cups unbleached flour

2 teaspoons baking powder

½ teaspoon salt

1 cup sugar

3 large eggs, beaten

3 tablespoons coconut oil

2 ½ teaspoons almond extract

¾ cup salted pistachios, shelled and coarsely chopped

1 cup craisins (dried cranberries)

3 ounces white chocolate, chopped

4 ounces white chocolate (for the icing)

Line a large baking sheet with parchment paper. In a medium bowl, combine flour, baking powder and salt. In a large bowl, combine sugar, eggs, coconut oil and almond extract. Add the flour mixture to the egg mixture and stir to combine. Add pistachios, craisins and chopped white chocolate. Mix well. Form the dough into a ball, wrap in plastic wrap, and chill for 30 minutes.

Preheat the oven to 350 degrees and remove the dough from the refrigerator. Divide the dough into two equal pieces, then shape them into two logs measuring about 2 inches in diameter and 12 to 14-inches long. Place logs on the parchment paper about 6 inches apart, giving them room for expansion during baking. Bake for 30 minutes. Cool for 30 minutes.

Reduce the oven temperature to 325 degrees. Place logs on a cutting board. Using a serrated knife, carefully slice them into ½-inch slices. Arrange the slices back on the parchment-lined baking sheet, baked sides down, and stagger the pieces to achieve a toasted texture on all sides. (Logs will be in the same position they were in before being cut but staggered to expose the sides to the oven heat. Keep standing up, do not lay flat.) Bake another 20 minutes, then cool until room temperature.

Break white chocolate into equally-sized pieces and place in the top of a double boiler. Fill the bottom of a double boiler with an inch or two of water and set the pan over low heat. Water in the bottom of the double boiler should never touch the top and should be a gentle boil. Stir chocolate frequently until melted. Remove chocolate from the heat as soon as it is melted and stir until smooth. Using a knife, butter top of each biscotti with white chocolate, then place on waxed paper to harden. This ensures a taste of white chocolate with every bite! Store in an air-tight container and freeze until ready to use.

Russian Tea Cakes

MAKES 70 SMALL COOKIES

Known as Mexican Wedding Cakes or Russian Tea Cakes, these cookies hit the spot every time. Buttery and flakey, they make a great addition to an afternoon coffee or are the perfect light dessert.

1/2 pound (2 sticks) butter, softened

1/2 cup confectioners' sugar

1 teaspoon vanilla extract

2 cups all-purpose, unbleached flour

1 cup salted almonds, chopped finely in food processor

Confectioners' sugar for rolling cookies

Preheat the oven to 325 degrees. In a large bowl and using an electric mixer, cream together butter, sugar and vanilla extract. Add flour and almonds and mix until blended. Roll dough into 70 small balls less than 1-inch in diameter.

On a baking sheet lined with parchment paper, place cookies and bake for 15 minutes, or until lightly golden. Remove from the oven, cool only slightly and then roll in confectioners' sugar. Transfer cookies to a wire cooling rack until totally cooled.

TIP: Serve in individual foil liners to dress them up, choosing a color to fit the occasion.

TIP: Confectioners' sugar, or powdered sugar, is used because it dissolves so quickly and results in a smooth texture.

Chocolate Dipped Strawberries

YIELDS ONE POUND OF DIPPED STRAWBERRIES

A double boiler and small kitchen scale are a must for this recipe. You can melt chocolate in the microwave; but if you do, the chocolate must be stirred every 30 seconds. Having a kitchen scale takes the guess work out of measurements. Mercken® chocolate is found in baking stores and yields a nice, shiny result.

4-ounces semisweet
Mercken® chocolate chips

16-ounces strawberries,
washed and dried thoroughly,
tops left on

Place the chocolate in the top of a double boiler. Fill the bottom of a double boiler with an inch or two of water and set the pan over low heat. Water in the bottom of the double boiler should never touch the top and should be a gentle boil. Stir chocolate frequently until melted. Turn off the burner once chocolate is melted but leave the double boiler on the burner.

Line a large, flat container with waxed paper. Set aside. Firmly hold the stem of strawberry and swirl it in the chocolate, coating the bottom half. Place dipped strawberry on waxed paper. Repeat until all strawberries and chocolate have been used.

Place strawberries in the refrigerator, UNCOVERED, for at least 45 minutes. Serve cold.

TIP: If the chocolate begins to thicken up, turn the heat back on under the double boiler and reheat chocolate at a low temperature. Add 1 teaspoon coconut oil to thin it out and stir to combine. Add more oil if necessary.

Sweet Espresso Almonds

MAKES 5 CUPS FLAVORED NUTS

These are a delicious, light after-dinner snack and make a fun hostess gift. For a festive look, buy the clear food bags at craft stores or specialty baking shops and dress the bags up with pretty ribbon.

½ cup granulated sugar

2 tablespoons espresso coffee beans, ground into a fine powder

1 tablespoon instant espresso coffee powder

½ teaspoon ground cinnamon

¼ teaspoon sea salt

1 large egg white

5 cups almonds, roasted and salted

Cooking spray

In a small bowl, combine sugar, espresso bean grounds, instant espresso coffee, cinnamon and salt.

Preheat the oven to 325 degrees. In a large bowl and using an electric mixer, beat egg white until frothy. Add almonds and toss to coat well. Add the espresso mixture to almonds and toss to coat well. Spray a jellyroll pan with cooking spray. Spread the coated nuts on the jellyroll pan and bake 5 minutes. With a spatula, loosen nuts, stir and bake another 5 minutes. Loosen nuts again. Place the jellyroll pan on a wire rack to cool. To store, place in an air-tight container and refrigerate.

TIP: Place the unused egg yolk in an air-tight container, refrigerate, and use the next morning in your scrambled eggs.

Mini Molten Chocolate Cakes

SERVES 12

For Valentine's Day, I use heart-shaped ramekins. I love this recipe because it can be made hours or even days in advance. Pop the cakes in the oven, sit down to dinner and they will be ready to serve when you are ready to enjoy them.

14-ounces semisweet chocolate chips

¾ cup butter

6 large eggs, separated

¼ teaspoon salt

1 cup granulated sugar

2 tablespoons coconut flour

½ teaspoon cayenne pepper (the secret ingredient)

12 fresh mint leaves for garnish

In the top of a double boiler, place chocolate chips and butter. Fill the bottom of a double boiler with an inch or two of water and set the pan over low heat. Water in the bottom of the double boiler should never touch the top and should be a gentle boil. Heat chocolate and butter until melted, stirring occasionally. Remove the top of the double boiler from the heat, mix chocolate and butter well and set aside, allowing mixture to cool down a bit.

Using an electric mixer and in a large bowl, place egg whites and salt and beat until foamy. Add sugar and continue beating until stiff peaks form. Set aside.

Quickly stir egg yolks into the chocolate mixture and continue stirring until blended, taking care yolks do not curdle. Add coconut flour and cayenne pepper and stir to combine. Gently fold the chocolate mixture into egg whites and blend.

Fill 12 (4-ounce) ovenproof ramekins 2/3 full with the chocolate mixture. Cover with plastic wrap and freeze at least 4 hours.

About 40 minutes before serving, preheat the oven to 325 degrees. Remove plastic wrap, place frozen ramekins on a baking sheet, and bake 30 minutes. Let cool 10 minutes before serving. Centers will be soft yet cooked with a slightly crackly top. Place a mint leaf on each cake for garnish. Serve warm.

TIP: If you really want to serve decadence, top cakes with whipped cream or vanilla bean ice cream.

Cookies and Cream Truffles

MAKES ABOUT 50 TRUFFLES

This super easy, no-bake dessert will disappear like magic. It has to be made ahead as two steps require chilling, so consider this recipe a last-minute time saver.

4 ½ sleeves Oreo® cookies, Double Stuffed variety (63 total cookies)

2 packages (16-ounces) cream cheese, softened

2 teaspoons vanilla extract

1 cup semisweet chocolate chips

or

1 cup white chocolate chips

or

½ cup semisweet and ½ cup white chocolate chips, melted separately

Reserved crushed cookies

In a food processor, crush 7 cookies and set aside. In the same food processor, finely crush the remaining 56 cookies. In a large bowl, place the 56 crushed cookies. Add cream cheese and vanilla. Mix well. Cover and chill in refrigerator until firm enough to shape into small balls, about 1 hour. Roll the cookie mixture into 1-inch balls. Cover and freeze for 2 hours.

Place the chocolate chips in the top of a double boiler. Fill the bottom of a double boiler with an inch or two of water and set the pan over a low heat. Water in the bottom of the double boiler should never touch the top and should be a gentle boil. Stir chocolate frequently until melted. Turn off the burner once chocolate is melted but leave the double boiler on the burner.

Dip frozen balls into melted chocolate, coating them well and allowing excess chocolate to drip back into the double broiler.

Place dipped truffles on a tray lined with waxed paper. Sprinkle with reserved crumbs. Cover and chill in the refrigerator for at least an hour before serving, longer if possible.

TO SERVE: Place truffles in individual, decorative mini-muffin liners and keep chilled until ready to serve.

TIP: I like the contrast of light and dark chocolates so I use both. If you choose to use two flavors, melt them separately. Dip half the truffles in dark and then dip the remaining in white.

Caramel Apple Fruit Dip

MAKES ABOUT 1 CUP OF DIP

This is so yummy for a brunch, Halloween dessert or just because! If there is any leftover dip by chance, try it the next morning spread on toast or a bagel.

FOR THE BOWL:

Small cantaloupe or in the fall, a small pumpkin for serving bowl

Using a "V"-shaped cutter, make a zig-zag pattern around the top third of cantaloupe by pushing the cutter into cantaloupe, pulling out, reinserting so that the zig-zag pattern runs evenly around the fruit, making sure the lines connect. Lift off the top third of cantaloupe and set aside. Using a spoon, scoop out seeds from larger cantaloupe section and chop into bite-sized pieces to use as dippers. If you don't have a "V"-shaped cutter, use a small knife to carve your zig-zag pattern, but the results are not as exact.

FOR THE CARAMEL DIP:

1 package (8-ounces) cream cheese, softened

½ cup brown sugar

1 teaspoon vanilla extract

¼ cup roasted, salted almonds, chopped

In a medium bowl, place cream cheese, brown sugar, vanilla and nuts and mix until well blended. Place the cream cheese mixture into the cantaloupe bowl. This may be prepared 24 hours in advance. Cover with plastic wrap and refrigerate until ready to serve.

FOR THE DIPPERS:

Some suggestions and quantities for fruit dippers:

1 pineapple (3 to 4 pounds) yields 40 chunks

1 honeydew melon (2 pounds) yields 36 chunks

3 medium apples (1 pound) yields 36 slices

TO SERVE: Place cantaloupe bowl in the center of tray and surround with a variety of fruit. Have toothpicks on hand for skewering the fruit.

TIP: If using apples, soak slices in lemon juice to keep them from turning brown.

Brownie and Strawberry Kabobs

MAKES 15 TO 20 KABOBS

*Mercken® chocolate can be found at a baking/cake decorating shop and online.
It heats up nicely and is shiny when it hardens.*

FOR THE BROWNIES:

Sugar for coating

4 ounces unsweetened chocolate

½ pound (2 sticks) butter or 1 cup coconut oil

5 large eggs, beaten

2 cups granulated sugar

1 teaspoon vanilla extract

¾ teaspoon ground cinnamon

¾ cup unbleached flour (add 1 tablespoon if at high altitude)

Cooking spray

Preheat the oven to 350 degrees. Line a 9 X 12-inch pan with parchment paper and spray the paper with cooking spray. Brownies will come out of the pan so much easier this way! Sprinkle sugar over the bottom and sides of the pan and shake to distribute.

Break the chocolate into equally-sized pieces and place in the top of a double boiler along with butter. Fill the bottom of a double boiler with an inch or two of water and set the pan over low heat. Water in the bottom of the double boiler should never touch the top and should reach a gentle boil. Stir the chocolate/butter mixture frequently until melted. Remove the top pan from the bottom and set the top aside until chocolate reaches room temperature.

In a large bowl and using an electric mixer, beat eggs and sugar until thick. Add vanilla and cinnamon and mix to combine. Using a large spoon, fold the chocolate mixture into the butter/sugar mixture and blend well.

Add flour to the chocolate mixture and fold until just blended using a spoon. Pour the batter into the prepared pan. Bake 30 minutes, or until knife inserted into center comes out clean, Cool on wire rack to room temperature before removing from the pan and cut into 1 ½-inch cubes.

Brownie Kabobs continued

TO ASSEMBLE KABOBS:

1 pound strawberries, washed, dried and stemmed

¼ pound dark Mercken® chocolate

¼ pound white Mercken® chocolate

Place strawberry, brownie cube and strawberry on 6-inch wooden skewers. Repeat until all strawberries have been used. Place filled skewers on a platter.

Line a large tray with waxed paper and set aside. Place each type of chocolate in a separate glass, microwavable, shallow dish. Place chocolates in the microwave, one flavor at a time, and cook in 30 seconds increments, stirring after every 30 seconds, until chocolate is liquid.

Using a large metal, slotted spoon, scoop up dark chocolate and gently shake the spoon until very fine threads come out the slots. Hold individual kabobs underneath falling chocolate and rotate kabobs, drizzling chocolate so that all sides are evenly sprinkled with threads of dark chocolate. Repeat this process with white chocolate. Place finished kabobs on waxed-paper lined tray, uncovered, until ready to serve.

Serving suggestion: Kabobs may be served on a tray or poked into a Styrofoam half ball. To serve on a Styrofoam ball, glue the ball to a plate with a glue gun, cover the half ball with spinach or lettuce leaves and poke the kabobs into the leaves, securing the leaves and covering the styrofoam This presentation is fun and gives height to your dessert. Styrofoam can be found at your favorite craft store.

TIP: If Mercken® chocolate cannot be found, use semisweet chocolate chips and white chocolate chips.

TIP: If the chocolate thickens up and will not drizzle, add a teaspoon of coconut oil at a time until it thins. DO NOT add water or the chocolate this clump and not be usable.

Vanilla Sugar

MAKES 1 CUP FLAVORED SUGAR

Turn this into a gift for the friend who loves lattes.
Package the sugar in a decorative spice container.

1 cup granulated sugar
1 vanilla bean

In a small bowl, place sugar. Using a paring knife, cut vanilla bean in half and then cut each halve lengthwise. Using a paring knife, scrap out seeds. Add seeds and both halves of vanilla bean to sugar. Toss to combine. Place the sugar mixture in an air-tight container for at least 2 weeks for flavors to blend. Leave the vanilla beans in the sugar until all the sugar is gone.

TIP: *Use vanilla sugar in coffee, atop rice pudding, sprinkled on tart fruits or in baking. The possibilities are endless.*

Rice Pudding

MAKES 1 ½ QUARTS PUDDING

Here's an updated version of a childhood favorite. Feel free to increase the amounts of raisins and cinnamon if you are a fan like I am.

Nonstick baking spray

1 cup uncooked basmati rice

¼ cup raisins

2 cups milk

1 large egg, beaten

1/3 cup granulated sugar

½ teaspoon vanilla extract

1 ½ teaspoon ground cinnamon

1/8 teaspoon salt

Cinnamon sticks

Vanilla sugar (See recipe on Page 183)

Preheat the oven to 335 degrees. Spray a 1½-quart ovenproof baking dish with nonstick baking spray. In a medium bowl, combine basmati rice, raisins, milk, egg, sugar, vanilla extract, cinnamon and salt. Pour the rice mixture into the baking dish.

Bake for 1 hour, stirring once after 30 minutes. Cool pudding on a metal cooling rack. Using a spoon, spoon pudding into 4-ounce dessert glasses. Sprinkle each dessert with the vanilla sugar. Using a kitchen torch, fan the torch over the sugar to caramelize the sugar, about 1 minute. Watch carefully. This can burn easily. Allow the topping to cool before serving. Place 1 cinnamon stick into each glass for garnish. Serve warm.

TIP: If you make this ahead to serve later, cover with plastic wrap and store in the refrigerator. Crystalize the vanilla sugar just before serving to add the crunch.

Festive Fruit Pizza

SERVES 10 TO 12

This dessert never gets old. For the Fourth of July, I like to make it with blueberries, raspberries and strawberries. For a Bronco football party, I use mandarin oranges and blueberries. Naturally, I use Christmas colors, red and green, in December. Be creative. For a non-holiday, use as many colors and shapes as possible to keep it interesting.

FOR THE COOKIE CRUST:

½ cup butter, softened

½ cup granulated sugar

½ cup confectioners' sugar

1 large egg

1 teaspoon vanilla extract

2 cups unbleached all-purpose flour*

3/8 teaspoon salt

½ teaspoon cream of tartar

½ teaspoon baking soda

½ cup oil (vegetable, canola, coconut)

In a large bowl and using an electric mixer, cream butter, sugars, egg and vanilla extract on medium speed until fluffy and light in color. In a medium bowl, combine flour, salt, cream of tartar and baking soda. With the mixer on low speed, slowly add dry ingredients to the wet ingredients. Slowly add oil and mix until combined. Form the dough into a flat disk, cover tightly with plastic wrap and refrigerate overnight or 8 hours.

TO COOK THE CRUST: Preheat the oven to 350 degrees. Remove chilled cookie dough from the refrigerator. Cover a 14-inch pizza pan with parchment paper. Press dough onto the pizza pan into a flat circle. Bake for 15 minutes, or until edges are very lightly browned. Allow crust to reach room temperature before decorating.

FOR THE TOPPINGS:

1 package (8-ounces) cream cheese, softened

½ cup confectioners' sugar

1 teaspoon vanilla extract

Assorted fresh fruit in a variety of colors

In a medium bowl and using an electric mixer, beat together cream cheese, sugar and vanilla extract on medium speed. Spread icing evenly over cooled sugar cookie crust, almost to the edge. Decorate top with sliced fruit as desired. Serve immediately or chill up to four hours until ready to serve.

*TIP: To make a gluten free option, substitute 2 cups of gluten-free flour for the all-purpose flour and add ½ teaspoon xanthan gum.

Bread Pudding with Rum Sauce

SERVES 8

This is delicious and, while normally served as a dessert, I even eat it for breakfast. Along with the rum sauce, I like topping it with whipped cream or vanilla ice cream.

FOR THE PUDDING:

½ loaf of your favorite bread (I like banana or cinnamon raisin, see recipe on next page)

2 tablespoons butter, melted

4 large eggs

1 cup milk

2/3 cup sugar

1 ½ teaspoons vanilla extract

Preheat the oven to 325 degrees. Using a pastry brush, brush 8 (5-inch) cast iron skillets with melted butter. Using a bread knife, slice bread into 1/2-inch cubes and arrange in skillets. In a medium bowl, place eggs, milk, sugar and vanilla and whisk to combine. Pour 1/8 of the egg mixture over bread cubes in each skillet. Bake for 30 to 40 minutes, or until firm/centers do not jiggle when moved.

FOR THE RUM SAUCE:

1/3 cup sugar

1 ½ teaspoons cornstarch

½ cup rum

Pinch of salt

1 ½ teaspoons butter

1 ½ teaspoons vanilla extract

In a small saucepan, combine sugar, cornstarch, rum and salt and stir to combine. Bring to a boil over low-medium heat, stirring constantly. Continue cooking for 2 minutes until the sauce thickens. Remove from the heat and add butter and vanilla. Stir to combine. Serve the Rum Sauce on the side.

Oatmeal Chocolate Chip Banana Bread

MAKES ONE LOAF BREAD

This is a family favorite for breakfast, a snack and also bread pudding. Warm up a slice with peanut butter and you have a meal! "Leftover banana bread" is an oxymoron with this recipe!

1 ½ cups flour (+2 tablespoons if at high altitude)

1 teaspoon salt

2 teaspoons baking powder

½ teaspoon baking soda

1 teaspoon cinnamon

¾ cups old fashioned oats

In a medium bowl, mix flour, salt, baking powder, baking soda, cinnamon and oats. Set aside.

½ cup coconut oil

2 eggs

½ cup sugar

1/3 cup buttermilk or soured milk

2/3 cup ripe bananas (about 2 medium bananas), mashed

½ cup semisweet chocolate chips

Preheat oven to 350 degrees. Prepare a loaf pan lined with parchment paper and sprayed with nonstick cooking spray.

In a large bowl, mix coconut oil, eggs, sugar, buttermilk, bananas and chocolate chips. Mix the flour mixture into the banana mixture and blend thoroughly. Pour batter into prepared loaf pan.

Bake 40-60 minutes and then cool for ten minutes on wire rack. Remove from loaf pan and finishing cooling on wire rack.

TIP: If buttermilk is not available, make soured milk by combining 1 teaspoon white vinegar, then add milk to equal 1/3 cup.

Spicy Crème Brûlée

SERVES 6

Crème Brûlée literally means "burnt cream". There are many variations of this dessert, and this is just one. It is a fun recipe to experiment with. You can't really go wrong if you use the basic ingredients. Just garnish it with fruit or serve it plain. Crème Brûlée should be made at least four hours before it is served.

2 cups heavy cream

1 large egg

4 large egg yolks

½ cup granulated sugar

1 teaspoon vanilla extract

½ teaspoon ground cinnamon

½ teaspoon ground cardamom

¼ teaspoon ground cloves

¼ teaspoon ground nutmeg

¼ teaspoon ground allspice

Pinch salt, less than 1/8 teaspoon

¼ cup granulated sugar for topping

Preheat the oven to 300 degrees. Place cream in the top of a double boiler. Fill the bottom of a double boiler with an inch or two of water and set the pan over low heat. Water in the bottom of the double boiler should never touch the top and should be a gentle boil. Heat cream until it almost reaches a boil. Remove the top of the double boiler from the bottom.

In a large bowl, place egg, egg yolks, sugar and vanilla and whisk to combine. Add cinnamon, cardamom, cloves, nutmeg, allspice and salt and whisk to combine. Whisk in warm cream quickly, taking care not to let the eggs curdle.

Pour the cream mixture into 6 (6-ounce) ramekins and set in an ovenproof baking pan with sides. Pour boiling water in baking pan until the water comes halfway up the sides of the ramekins. Place the baking pan in the oven and bake about 40 minutes, or until the custard is softly set. Remove the ramekins from the water bath and refrigerate for at least 4 hours. Do not cover ramekins until the custard is chilled. Cover with plastic wrap if chilling for longer than 4 hours.

Sprinkle each dish with 1/6 of the sugar. Using a kitchen torch, fan the torch over the sugar to caramelize the sugar, about 1 minute. Watch carefully. This can burn easily. Allow the topping to cool before serving.

TIP: *For extra fluffy scrambled eggs, refrigerate those extra 4 egg whites in an air-tight container and add them to your eggs the following morning.*

Monster Cookies

MAKES 60 LARGE COOKIES

I make my Monster Cookies with old-fashioned oats, not quick oats. And, yes, this recipe contains no flour. It makes enough to feed a large crowd. If you have any leftovers, these cookies freeze well. One Monster Cookie fan suggested the only thing better than a Monster Cookie is two Monster Cookies with ice cream sandwiched in between. I can't disagree.

1 cup butter, softened

2 cups granulated sugar

2 cups brown sugar

6 large eggs

1 jar (24-ounces) peanut butter, smooth or crunchy

1 tablespoon vanilla extract

1 teaspoon cinnamon

4 teaspoons baking soda

½ teaspoon salt

9 cups old-fashioned oats

1 ¼ cups M & M's® chocolate candies

1 1/3 cups semisweet chocolate chips

or

1 ¼ cups combination M & M's® chocolate candies and white chocolate chips

1 ½ cups nuts, chopped, optional

Preheat a conventional oven to 350 degrees. If using a convection oven, preheat it to 335 degrees.

In a very large bowl and using a wooden spoon, cream together butter and sugars. Beat in eggs, peanut butter and vanilla. Add cinnamon, baking soda, salt and oats and mix well. Add M & M®'s, chocolate chips and nuts and mix well.

Using an ice cream scoop, scoop up dough and place on a parchment-lined cookie sheet about 4-inches apart. One cookie sheet should hold 6 cookies. Flatten dough with the palm of your hand. Bake 11 to 15 minutes, or until cookies are lightly golden. Cool 3 minutes on the baking sheet, then transfer cookies to a wire cooling rack. Store in an air-tight container for up to 1 week.

TIP: Saigon Cinnamon is the most flavorful and my favorite. It can be found in specialty spice stores. I also prefer Mexican Vanilla as it has the most intense vanilla flavor, also found in specialty spice shops.

Useful Cooking Trivia and Tips

- Avocados are a fruit with more potassium than a banana. It is a myth that placing the pit in guacamole will prevent darkening. How to remove the pit - cut avocado in half lengthwise and firmly hold half with pit in one hand and quickly strike pit with sharp chef's knife. Twist the knife to loosen and then remove the pit.

- Butter used in my recipes is salted butter.

- A Double Boiler is basically a pot within a pot. The insert nests in a pot with an inch or two of water but does not touch the upper insert. The water boils and heats up the upper pot, preventing burning as the heat is indirect. Do not let the water dry up!

- When my recipe calls to set aside an onion or pepper for another recipe, do this: chop it up and freeze in a zipper bag. Defrosting really isn't necessary as it will thaw quickly.

- Never put eggshells down a garbage disposal. Why not? Because the little pieces stick to the sides of the pipes, eventually narrowing the passage and clogging up the system.

- Julienne-style vegetables are just thin, matchstick-size slices of a vegetable like carrots and zucchini. Purchase a julienne tool and you will look like a professional.

- Invest in a professional kitchen torch for Crème Brulee and charring peppers.

- I love my mandoline to slice perfectly even slices of vegetables, but always use the guard to hold the vegetable. This device is sharp, trust me!

- Bring meats to room temperature before cooking, preventing them from sticking to the cooking surface. For food safety purposes, leave out of refrigerator no longer than one hour.

- You need an oven thermometer! Most ovens beep at the set temperature but it isn't really there! Hence the need to preheat the oven in my recipes.

- Parchment paper is a staple along with aluminum foil. Use parchment paper to line cookie sheets and loaf pans, aluminum foil to line baking sheets for brussels sprouts.

- Washing all produce is really important to prevent bacteria from entering via the knife.

- Zest is the grated skin of a lemon, lime or orange. A special grating device may be purchased for this purpose. I own several!

Index by category

Index by category (continued)

Index in alphabetical order

Index in alphabetical order (continued)